RENEWING
THE FAMILY SPIRIT

Overcoming Conflict to Enjoy Stronger Family Ties

David J. Ludwig

Publishing House
St. Louis

This book is dedicated to my wife, Kathy,
whose vibrant, loving spirit has kept
our family spirit very much alive.

Copyright © 1989 Concordia Publishing House
3558 S. Jefferson Avenue, St. Louis, MO 63118-3968
Manufactured in the United States of America.

Library of Congress Cataloging-in-Publication Data
Ludwig, David J.
    Renewing the family spirit: overcoming conflict to enjoy stronger family ties/David J. Ludwig.
        p. cm.—(Good news for families. Renewing the family spirit series)
        ISBN 0-570-04527-4
        1. Family—Religious life. I. Title. II. Series.
BV4526.2.L83 1989
248.4—dc20   89-32286
                                                                          CIP

1 2 3 4 5 6 7 8 9 10   98 97 96 95 94 93 92 91 90 89

Contents

Preface   5
Chapter 1   Atmospheric Conditions   10
             within the Family
Chapter 2   The Home Environment: 24
             Taking a Turn for Better
             or for Worse
Chapter 3   Turbulence: When   42
             Personalities Clash like
             High- and Low-Pressure
             Systems
Chapter 4   Deeper Turbulence: 62
             The Clash of Powerful
             Sexual and Parental
             Emotions
Chapter 5   Critical Turbulence: 78
             The Power of Different
             Backgrounds Clashing
Chapter 6   Beyond Turbulence: 94
             Breaking the Stagnation
             of a Bad Spirit
Chapter 7   Living in the Right   112
             Spirit: The Strong Force
             Creates Fair Weather for
             the Family
Chapter 8   Renewing Your Family's   126
             Spirit: God in Control of
             the Weather in Your
             Home

Preface

The Spirit!
"Esprit de corps!"
"School spirit!"
"I won't be there physically, but I'll be there in spirit!"
"They were all in such good spirits!"
"He's such a bad-spirited person!"
These are all common uses of the word *spirit* today.
And there are many more.

"Where two or three come together in my name, there
am I *with* them" (Matt. 18:20). God's presence is real. His
Spirit is with us in all that we do. But how real does the
Holy Spirit seem to Christians today?

Our culture tries to reduce everything to simple facts.
We are taught to look for physical causes. Christ's presence
as "the unseen guest at every meal" seemed much more
real 40 years ago as I was growing up than it does today.
I still remember setting an extra place for Him at the table.
I would be excited imagining that Jesus was actually sitting
next to me.

With our narrow sense of reality today, such a vivid
sense of the spiritual seems almost out of place. Spiritual
forces and truths are still as real and as present as in Biblical
days, but the world, with some help from the devil, has
worn away our ability—and maybe even our desire—to
see the spiritual around us.

This book is meant to sharpen the modern Christian's
vision of the spiritual. Powerful, unrelenting forces are at
work between people as they struggle to relate to each
other. These forces are deep and mysterious. They are
expressed in the powerful give-and-take of our relationships. This happens where people are connected by a

shared spirit, in which what goes on is unseen yet all-important.

Christians as well as non-Christians need to recognize one of the basic premises of this book: the reality of the spiritual. Modern psychology often ignores the spiritual dimension in relationships. Our approach challenges that omission. Christians also often overlook this spiritual dimension in their daily lives. Satisfied with a traditional verbalizing of the Gospel, they tend to forget the sanctifying power of the Holy Spirit, invisible to be sure, but always present. Without the sustaining power of the Holy Spirit the Christian cannot even remain in the faith, much less live a happy, faithful life. It is a major goal of this book to help families acknowledge and receive the support of the Spirit every day of their lives.

You can begin to sharpen your spiritual senses. You might put an extra chair at your table to remind yourself of the reality of Jesus as your unseen guest. In the same way, you can "set a place" for the Spirit to be present throughout the day at the places where the lives of people meet. This preparation can help you recall the reality of the spiritual connections in your life.

This book will chart the *shared spirit* that connects members of the family. You will develop insight into how to work on the *family ties* that are realized through these special spiritual connections.

An important key in developing these insights is understanding the resulting disposition between family members—the spirit or atmosphere of the home, especially as Satan struggles to win over that spirit. The *shared spirit* of the family reflects the history of its relationships. It also expresses the quality of contact that takes place between family members. If the shared spirit is free and clear, contact is easy and good. This is a gift of the Holy Spirit in reconciliation.

But if misunderstanding accumulates between family members, the shared spirit becomes heavy and bogged down. It no longer flows freely in that space. Good feelings are replaced with moodiness and suspicion. As the space between them clutters up, the atmosphere becomes even more tense and cold. The devil grabs this opportunity to reinforce the things that grieve the Holy Spirit. "Get rid of all bitterness, rage and anger, brawling and slander, along with every form of malice" (Eph. 4:31).

This book looks at differences between people. Differences can divide, or they can be the basis for making good spiritual connections. Differences in the way you were raised, your personality, and your gender are usually the sources of misconnections. Suggestions are given to help "clear the air," which we can compare to weather patterns. Cleared air keeps the shared spirit free of the stalled atmospheric patterns that pull down the mood of the home.

I write this book because I am convinced that marriage and family relationships—and all relationships for that matter—can be much more alive and healthy. But individuals need to know how to renew the family spirit. I have yet to find a couple say to me, "Yes, when we got married, we wanted our relationship to break apart. We worked at destroying it." Yet in subtle but powerful ways that they themselves did not realize, the two people—along with other forces—actually did work at destroying the fresh, positive, and healthy atmosphere that God intended. Perhaps Jesus' words on the cross would be applicable: "Father, forgive them, for they do not know what they are doing" (Luke 23:34).

This book is aimed at family relationships—traditional, single-parent, and blended families. We have described family settings that are typical of what most people experience. Throughout the book we refer to the Christian faith and to Scriptural insights into the "things unseen" and the workings of the Holy Spirit. We affirm the solid Biblical foundation of marital fidelity in the family with husband/wife and parent/children relationships and order according to God's plan. Not everything can be said on the subject within these few pages, but we strongly affirm the Biblical emphasis on the importance of sound family structure and relationships.

Our discussion deals with the sanctified life, built on justification—on the work of Jesus Christ to forgive sins. God has reconciled the world to Himself. We are reconciled to God. Based on that reconciliation, we offer forgiveness to our family members as we deal with our differences in an ongoing way. As we live in forgiveness, the spirit of family is renewed and grows. We are set free from blaming others when the home environment breaks down. Realizing that we are all sinful, we are brought to our knees together, asking God to help us renew a right spirit within our family and home.

This book can also be used as part of a family educational experience. Questions begin each chapter. They are meant to be used privately or in a group setting. A video program based on this book is also available for a family group experience.

This book is not intended to solve serious problems without professional help. It is aimed at strengthening basically sound relationships. Healthy families often need guidelines to help them develop into even stronger families. And the need today is great!

Before You Read Chapter 1

Have you . . .

. . . ever wondered what holds a family together?
Look at Ephesians 4:15–16.
Where are the "joints" that hold your family together?
Go over in your mind all the relationships within your
family. Are any of them "out of joint"?

. . . ever heard of a family spirit?
Look at John 3:8.
Did you know that *spirit* literally means "wind" or
"movement of air"? Test the atmosphere of your
home. Is there fair weather, or do you sense a storm
brewing?

. . . ever felt a good spirit?
Look at Galatians 5:22.
"Love," "joy," and "peace" sure sound like a good
atmosphere to me! Wouldn't you rather live with a
good spirit at home? Imagine being with a good friend.
Test the atmosphere between the two of you—warm,
sunny, and peaceful.

. . . ever felt a bad spirit?
Look at Galatians 5:19–20.
Do these sound like healthy family emotions to you?
Imagine being with someone you do not trust at all.
Test the air—cold, hostile, and stagnant!

. . . ever felt a troubled or turbulent spirit?
Look at John 13:21.
Have feelings ever been hurt around your home? It
felt like a frontal system came through and changed
the weather, didn't it—leaving turbulence, upset, and
hurt.

Chapter 1

Atmospheric Conditions within the Family

Dawn was watching TV in the family room with Rose, her sister, and Sonny, her brother. Robert and Elaine, their parents, were lounging on the sofa, paging through the evening newspaper. Suddenly Dawn shrieked with delight. "Mommy, Daddy, look! There's a beautiful balloon going up in the air! And people are riding in a little basket! See! Can we go for a balloon ride, please?" Dawn was clearly excited. She looked back and forth between her father and mother, wrinkling her nose as she always did when she expressed her delight. Rose and Sonny perked up at the idea and excitedly joined in. Robert and Elaine looked at each other, and a special warmth linked them together. They shared a glowing moment of love as they became a part of their children's enthusiasm.

The Spring family, like other families, is held together by connections that transmit feelings of warmth and love between family members. These connections can be called the family "ties." St. Paul refers to these ties in the following passage:

Speaking the truth in love, we will in all things grow up into him who is the Head, that is, Christ. From him the whole *body, joined and held together* by every supporting ligament, grows and builds itself up in love. (Eph. 4:15–16)

St. Paul uses an analogy of a physical body connected at the joints by tendons and ligaments. In the body of the family there are connecting points between each member of the family where invisible "tendons" and "ligaments" join the family together. The relationships between family members make up these connecting places.

When each of these "joints" is working properly, the family members enjoy and share their lives with each other. The family then "builds itself up in love." But when one of the ligaments is "out of joint," the family no longer works as it was meant to. This crippling effect is caused by bad relationships—between husband and wife, parents and children, or among children.

Relationships make up the family ties. And relationships, like the body, are extremely complex. They are an important part of the spiritual life. In the area where family members are "joined and held together," invisible yet powerful forces are at work. These forces affect the mood of the family. You can almost see the forces between family members when they are with each other. They are sometimes positive and wholesome, sometimes tentative and uncertain, and at times they are negative and destructive. What's more, these forces can shift and flow like the wind. They bring freshness and crispness to a relationship, or they build up in deadening stagnation.

Let's take a look at these forces as they move about in Robert and Elaine's life.

A Good Atmosphere

The party was fun. Robert was thoroughly enjoying himself, telling jokes and kidding around with friends. He felt free and energetic, full of witty comments and clever ideas. Elaine was also having a good time. She was in a good mood. Much of the time there was a group of people around her, listening to her tell story after

11

story about the children with whom she worked. It was obvious that others enjoyed being around her. As they left, several people commented that they were a terrific couple to be around.

The Atmosphere Changes

The good mood continued as they drove home. Elaine sat close to Robert and teased him about showing off. They were still teasing and kidding when Elaine opened the glove compartment to see if one of her combs was still there. She caught a glimpse of a credit card receipt crumpled in the back corner. She pulled it out and glanced at it. Suddenly her stomach tightened into a knot. Her whole demeanor changed. A sudden coolness settled in. She demanded in an icy tone, "Where did this come from? Did you charge something behind my back again?" A heaviness descended on Robert's chest. He sighed, not believing that Elaine could bring up a sensitive subject like money when they had been having so much fun. Robert settled uncomfortably back into himself. Getting no response, Elaine also became frustrated and quiet. The uneasy silence held all the way home. It was as if an invisible force had come between them, dramatically shifting the mood.

A Bad Atmosphere Settles In

Elaine broke the silence when they got home. "Well, it looks like you spent more money . . ." she began with a note of hurt in her voice. Robert looked coldly at her. With a shrug of his shoulders, he spoke in controlled, measured words, "I just put some money down on a hot air balloon ride for the whole family, but as usual you've ruined the fun of it." Now bitterness swelled in Robert's voice, laced with a strong dose of resentment. Elaine got the message. She stiffened and looked at Robert. With fire in her eyes, she spoke through clenched teeth: "Me? Why don't you take a good look at yourself for a change?" She seemed like a snake coiled to strike.

What's going on here? One moment Robert and Elaine are warm and close and the next they are cold and distant. Later they are angry and poised for more deadly conflict. Mysterious changes like these in the home atmosphere express what goes on between family members. It is easy to talk when the atmosphere is good. But when the climate shifts and there is tension in the air, a rigid silence takes over and little, if anything, can be shared.

What has the power to take a delightful atmosphere and turn it into a tense, frustrating one? Just what is it that controls the mood of the home?

What Controls the Atmosphere?

Neither Robert nor Elaine wanted the mood to shift when they left the party. It was not their intention to spend the rest of the evening in a hostile climate. Yet when the atmosphere changed, neither had the power to change it back into a good mood by an act of will. There was a force present when they were alone, a force so powerful that it blocked their communication and set the mood for the rest of the evening.

This force controls the "atmosphere" of the home. An atmosphere exists between people. It is where the family ties connect individuals within a family. Since this force is so powerful and seems to have a will of its own, we can describe it best as a *spiritual* force.

The word for *spirit* (spelled with a small *s*) in both Hebrew and Greek means "movement of air," "wind," or

13

"breath." Like the wind that "blows wherever it pleases," spiritual forces are unseen and intangible. But they are real and powerful. Scripture uses the analogy of wind to describe the work of God's Spirit on our spirits. You can "hear its sound, but you cannot tell where it comes from or where it is going" (John 3:8). Sometimes that force becomes "a sound like the blowing of a violent wind" (Acts 2:2). At other times it is a simple wind caused by a breath of air (John 20:22).

Your spirit can be described as the atmosphere within you. If you are in good spirits, the atmosphere inside is sunny, warm, and bright. We say that you are in an "up" mood. But if your spirit changes, the atmosphere inside can become dark and stormy. You become caught in a "down" mood.

Your spirit can be raised by the good atmosphere of a loving, caring community (2 Cor. 7:13; Rom. 1:11–12). In the same way, the bad atmosphere of an individual will negatively affect the group spirit. These spiritual forces interact with each other in a powerful way.

The Shared Spirit Controls the Atmosphere

When two family members meet, their lives overlap. The overlap is the *shared spirit* of the two people. This shared spirit is the dynamic, changing quality and flow of the relationship between people. It was formed by all that has gone into the relationship in the past. This shared spirit not only influences but actually *controls the atmosphere* between Robert and Elaine. Since it cannot be seen, it is easy to overlook or deny its existence. But such an unseen force living in the connecting place between them is real and long-lasting.

You can imagine that shared spirit as living in the space between people, expressing and in a strange way controlling their interaction. When the atmosphere is good, the relationship is open and easy. But when the atmosphere turns cloudy and stormy, the relationship breaks down.

Weather Patterns

To understand the home environment better, imagine yourself watching a TV weatherman explain what is happening. Notice that there are warm and sunny areas on the weather map. Then a frontal system moves across the screen, bringing a change in the weather. Elsewhere, bad weather strikes.

Weather is created by different systems of pressure coming into contact. Low pressure meets high pressure. Cool air meets warm moist air. Weather happens along the front where they come together. This activity develops out of the differences between the air masses. It may result in a refreshing or beneficial change. Or the clash of fronts may cause considerable disturbance and even destruction.

The dramatic shift in mood that took place between Robert and Elaine was like a change in the weather. One minute it was warm and sunny. But a disagreement based on differences between Robert and Elaine suddenly caused a front to move in. The atmosphere chilled, bringing stormy and turbulent times. Bad weather then dominated the atmosphere of their relationship.

A Good Spirit—What God Intends

A good atmosphere involves living "by the Spirit" (Gal. 5:16). God intends for us to live happy, fulfilled lives as part of His family. His gift of the Holy Spirit makes this possible. His Spirit has the power to create and sustain a good spirit in our lives. "The fruit of the Spirit is love, joy, peace, patience, kindness, goodness, faithfulness, gentleness and self-control" (vv. 22–23).

A good spirit shows up in the atmosphere of your home. Remember the last time your family was having fun together. Didn't you feel free and expressive, with good energy flowing between family members? Didn't the atmosphere of that shared spirit feel warm and inviting, like a beautiful spring day? You can relax in such an atmosphere.

The Atmosphere of a Good Spirit—
Enjoy the Good Atmosphere!

Remember Robert and Elaine at the party. They were relaxed and open with their friends. Their facial expressions conveyed different emotions as they talked. Their hands freely added just the right emphasis. Their voices easily expressed their feelings and reactions. Good eye contact emphasized their involvement with others. When it was time to leave, they were not really ready to go but felt like lingering in that good atmosphere.

A Bad Spirit—So What's New?

We know that differences between people are natural, even expected. God created us as unique individuals. Our personalities, our gender, and our own personal histories accentuate the differences. These differing mixtures that make each of us unique are like weather patterns. When two systems meet, they will do one of three things. (1) They will merge easily, and a good flow will take place. (2) They will deepen and resist one another. Clashes will inevitably happen. (3) They may become stagnant and blocked. Their relationship will develop into a stalemate.

The bad atmosphere is a blocked system that causes dead, stale air. It originates with the force of evil ("the ruler of the *kingdom of the air*" Eph. 2:2). He has been around for a long, long time. His influence causes stagnation in our lives. His power acts like an inversion, blocking out fresh, clean air. The devil nourishes our natural desires to do what is contrary to God's Spirit (Gal. 5:17). "The acts of the sinful nature are obvious: . . . hatred, discord, jealousy, fits of rage . . ." (vv. 19–20). These acts inflict heavy damage.

We should not be surprised by this force of evil in our lives and our relationships. It is as close and as commonplace as the bad feelings that occur between members of our own family.

16

Can you remember a situation in your life when the mood was really bad? One person truly intended to hurt another. He or she may have wanted to hurt the other person's feelings or even hurt the other physically or in some other way. What did it feel like? Didn't you feel the hostility and the bad atmosphere? It probably felt extremely tense and heavy with threat!

The Atmosphere of a Bad Spirit— Run for Cover!

For Robert and Elaine the hostile atmosphere settled in after they came home. It influenced both of them to be hard and bitter toward each other. Neither would trust what the other said. Their faces became rigid. Their expressions changed dramatically, and each wore a look of disgust. Their voices were guarded, and the words came out measured with a definite cutting edge to them. Their eyes simmered with repressed anger. A tender touch at that moment would be rejected—even resented.

A Front Blows In—The Changing Weather

But how did their warm atmosphere turn cold and hostile? A frontal system drove through to disrupt the good weather. For Robert and Elaine it developed with the accidental discovery of the credit card slip. This discovery set off a sudden storm that led to a breakdown of communication. The good spirit was broken between them.

Since agitated and confused communication results from this frontal system, we can describe the changing weather as a *turbulent spirit*. The wholeness of a good spirit and the unity that it expresses is broken. The overlap of mutual understanding splinters. The shared spirit divides into two contending, individual spirits. Jesus came to unite people as part of God's family. But as Scripture vividly describes, even while Jesus spoke of the unity that He had with His disciples, the thought of Judas's betrayal of Jesus shattered that unity. Jesus was left "troubled in spirit" (John 13:20–21).

Remember a family situation when things were going along smoothly but then something happened. The communication suddenly broke down, leaving everyone feeling frustrated and misunderstood. Didn't the atmosphere feel confused and turbulent? Perhaps the change took you by surprise, leaving you puzzled as to why it happened.

The Atmosphere of a Turbulent Spirit—
Watch Out! Turbulence Ahead

When Elaine first discovered the receipt for the hot-air balloon ride and confronted Robert with it, their systems collided head-on. The openness and ease of conversation changed into a guarded, uncertain silence. Both were frustrated and hurt. Neither wanted the pleasant mood to shift to a negative one. But both immediately felt the consequences of the change in the weather.

A Deeper Look at the Turbulent Spirit

We should not be surprised that negative or bad patterns develop in our lives. It has happened throughout history and will continue to happen. The most important issue is what God would have us do about it.

The turbulent spirit is the changing atmospheric condition. A frontal system suddenly turned good weather between Robert and Elaine into bad weather. That bad weather may stagnate and continue for some time. The differences between Robert and Elaine may go unresolved. The front may just stall.

But there is hope! A new system may push through. Differences may be confronted and resolved. Hard and bitter feelings that develop between family members may be worked out, even if it means living in a turbulent atmosphere for a while.

Although turbulence feels unsettling and unpleasant,

it is the creative edge of relationships. Clashes stemming from differences between family members create this unsettled atmosphere. These differences provide the continued energy to keep the relationships interesting and exciting.

You may not be able to do much about the weather outside your home. But think of Ben Franklin who learned about electricity from a lightening storm. You can learn something from the storms that brew inside your home. And what's more important, by the power of God's Holy Spirit something can be done about the weather inside your home.

Chapter 1: Weather Watch Activities

(*Note:* These activities are designed to put the concepts of the chapter to work in your life. There are many ways you can work through these activities. You can do them by yourself, either by keeping a journal or by working them through in your head. You can do them with other members of your family. Or you can do them within a group setting.)

1. Think of the last time you were with a good friend. Test the atmosphere between you. Think of words that describe the spirit of your friendship. Add to the following list:

warm   open   energizing

2. What happened to your spirit after you left this good atmosphere? Add to the following list of words that describe the lingering effect of a good spirit:

uplifting   wholesome   relaxing

3. Imagine yourself in the presence of someone you would rather not have to face. Test the atmosphere of this

relationship. Think of words that would describe the atmosphere and add to the following list:

cold   bitter   hostile

4. What happens to your spirit after you leave this bad atmosphere? Add to the following list of words that describe the lingering effects of a bad spirit:

depressing   hardening   unhealthy

5. Think of a time this past week when communication with someone suddenly got confusing. Test this atmosphere. Think of words that would describe your turbulent spirit and add to the following list:

confused   frustrating   unsettled

6. Think of the various people you have been with during the past day. Test the atmosphere in each situation. Was the mood light and uplifting (▲) or unsettled and confusing (≈), or was there some sign of a bad spirit (▼)? Think of how the atmosphere affected communication or interaction between people.

7. Keep track of each person you encounter during this next day. Test the atmosphere and decide how to describe the mood or atmosphere. Was it light and uplifting (▲), leaving you free to express yourself? Was it cold and depressing (▼) as you realized that you do not trust each other? Was it unsettled and frustrating (≈), leaving you confused about the communication?

8. Observe people's body language in each of the three atmospheres. What differences do you see in eye contact, freedom of movement, and voice tone? What about touch? Can you even imagine touching in the atmosphere of a bad spirit (▼)?

9. Keep track of your own spirit (the atmosphere within) during this next day. Chart the shifts of your mood

in an up and down fashion. Note how your spirit is affected by the different atmospheres that you encounter and by the different thoughts that you have.

10. Think of the mood shifts that have taken place in your home this past week. Put up your finger and test the atmoshphere as it changed. Describe each mood as good (▲), bad (▼) or changing (≈).

11. What causes the atmosphere to shift at your house? Think of situations that will predictably bring about a change in mood. What topic (such as money, friends, in-laws) can bring a frontal system through quickly?

12. Think of each of your family members in turn. Put up your finger to test the atmosphere between the two of you. Is there a good spirit (▲) there? Are there bad feelings (▼)? Or would you just call things turbulent (≈) at the moment?

13. Now think of how different members of your family relate to each other. Put up your finger to test the atmosphere in each case. Which of these apply: a good spirit (▲), a bad spirit (▼), or a turbulent spirit (≈)?

14. Do the same with the relationships where you work or even with some of the more important relationships within your church. Which symbol is most appropriate in each case?

Notes

1. The idea of a figurative "shared space" between two people as one way to conceptualize the working of spiritual forces is similar to Kurt Lewin's description of "personal space" that makes up the basis for the individual's perception of life (*Principles of Topological Psychology* [New York: McGraw-Hill, 1936]). As this concept of the

forces that affect perception (vectors and valences in Lewin's terms) is applied to the shared space between two people, it becomes an exciting analogy that puts life and immediacy into the concept of spiritual forces that are at work within relationships and within families.

2. The disciplines of psychology and sociology no longer have appropriate words for the forces that affect the mood or the atmosphere of an individual or of a situation. Since the word *spirit* dropped out of usage in psychological literature, only more bland terms such as "emotional tone" or "motivational climate" remain to describe this powerful force. The word *spirit* is the most accurate way to describe this felt but unseen force that controls the atmosphere of the family.

3. Forces that control the atmosphere of the family or the mood of an individual are puzzling to many people. Perhaps the perception of such unseen and intangible forces has been blurred through the scientific pursuit of the observable and measurable. Our society seems to have opted for specialized knowledge and tangible solutions at the expense of the deeper spiritual realities. Heightened awareness of the existence of the unseen, intangible areas of life where the vital connections take place will help people treat the spiritual once again with awe and respect.

4. Personal salvation and the individual's relationship with God is the focus of much of today's religion. A reading of the New Testament shows constant concern for the community and the family of God. Perhaps this focus on the individual is why the ability to discern spiritual forces that exist "when two of three are gathered together" is not a common concept today.

Before You Read Chapter 2

Have you . . .

. . . ever wondered why people deliberately hurt each
other?
Read Genesis 37:2–11.
Joseph's brothers were out to get him, and their resentment gradually turned into something destructive? Feelings "stick" from one situation to the next.
Think for a minute—are you holding a grudge against
another family member? I bet you are!

. . . ever gone to bed angry?
Look at Ephesians 4:26–27.
Watch out! Anger can turn into sin. Think of some-
thing this past week that hurt you. Is it still there?

. . . ever thought that anger was good?
Look at Exodus 4:10–17.
God got angry for a good purpose. Think of the last
time you were depressed. At whom were you angry?
It's this simple: Hold anger in and stagnate; express
it cleanly and energize your relationships.

. . . ever thanked God for turbulence in your life?
Look at Matthew 5:23–25.
Turbulence handled right can lead to deeper relation-
ship. We're talking Christian lifestyle!

Chapter 2

The Home Environment: Taking a Turn for Better or for Worse

Weather patterns develop in the shared spirit between family members. Where do these powerful patterns come from—patterns that can shift the atmosphere of a whole family?

After their bitter exchange, Elaine tried to make contact again. "Look," she ventured, "I'm sorry the money situation came up." Robert tried to lighten the mood again, "Well, I guess we can agree to disagree." But Elaine stiffened and shot back, "I'm sorry, but this is more than a disagreement. You tried to hide that charge slip from me!" And turbulence swirled back into their life once again as Robert stomped out of the kitchen.

When two people walk away from each other, a charged atmosphere remains between them, reflecting the mood. When they come back together, the memory of the previous mood is still there. And what's more, this memory of similar situations accumulates over time. These charged remnants are like particles that accumulate from one situation to another. We will call them "IMPs," which stands for "Illusive Mood Particles." These are particles or remnants of feelings or moods—that is, particles of the mood left behind to influence the next meeting.

These mood particles cannot be seen, but their presence is unmistakable. They exist between two people as shared memories of previous moods. It is as if the mood of a charged interaction is captured in this particle that sticks in the shared space. Something has now "come between" the two people.

Isolated, these mood particles do not seem important. But the same frustration and miscommunication can occur again and again.

This lets the mood particles accumulate and band together. Collectively they become Intensified Mood Particles that layer or build up. After a period of time, they become strong, mood-controlling forces in the relationship. In some ways they are massive and immovable. If the IMPs are positive and soaring, it will take a lot to damage the good feelings. If they are negative, they develop strong negative feelings that remain until they are broken up.

> Robert and Elaine had to deal with their IMPs:
> After Robert retreated into the garage, he sat dejected at his workbench. "Why does she always have to harp on money?" he muttered to himself. "She just goes on and on until everything's upset." He settled into his anger. Every time he replayed the scene in his mind, the anger perked up again. Several minutes passed, and things began to settle down inside. Robert resolved to be more pleasant. He walked into the house with a determined smile on his face. He started to say something. But when he caught Elaine's eye, the tension rushed back. He turned and angrily marched off to bed. When Elaine came to bed a little later, they carefully avoided touching each other. An invisible wall seemed to have sprung up between them.

IMPs are a major part of relationships. The turbulent atmosphere stuck in the space between Robert and Elaine when Robert retreated into the garage. When he came back into the kitchen, it remained even though he tried to will it away. The tension continued through the night.

The IMPs that build up in Robert and Elaine's shared space are like a random thunderstorm. A tiny but powerful storm filled with energy stays between them. As it becomes part of the shared spirit, it affects future weather patterns until something causes it to dissipate.

IMPs Left in the Shared Space

As they build up around issues such as work, money, discipline, and others, IMPs become the history of the relationship. Collectively, they are forces affecting the future weather patterns in Elaine and Robert's life.

If Robert and Elaine walk away in a good mood, an invisible *fair weather sign* (▲) remains in the shared space to indicate the *updraft* of a good spirit. This pattern will be there the next time they meet. This is a soaring IMP.

When they go their own ways bitter and hostile, a bad spirit remains behind. A *stagnant weather pattern* (▼)— an atmospheric *inversion* or downdraft—hovers in that space. This is a fiendish or demonic IMP.

If they withdraw in the confusion and hurt of a turbulent spirit, an invisible *changing pattern* (≈) occupies that space. This is the mischievous IMP.

A Weather Map of the Shared Space

Now it's possible to make a weather chart for Robert and Elaine, picturing the spiritual forces that exist in their connecting space. For simplicity, let's divide the space into three different areas.

In the following chart these are family time, discipline, and money. We'll mark each area with the symbol that represents the IMPs left in that space each time they parted.

Since the good mood *uplifts* the spirit, put the fair or soaring IMPs (▲) toward the upper part of the chart.

If the mood is in the *downdraft* of the stagnant atmosphere, put the inversion (▼) or fiendish IMP toward the bottom.

Put the symbol for changing or turbulent weather (≈) in the middle of the chart, since it is mischievous and may move either up or down.

Weather Chart

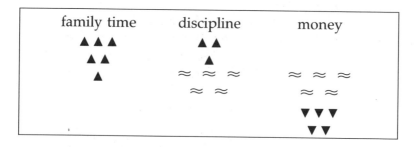

family time	discipline	money
▲ ▲ ▲	▲ ▲	
▲ ▲	▲	
▲	≈ ≈ ≈	≈ ≈ ≈
	≈ ≈	≈ ≈
		▼ ▼ ▼
		▼ ▼

This chart shows the IMPs that have accumulated invisibly in three major areas of Robert and Elaine's shared space. When Robert and Elaine work around the house together or spend time together, they usually leave each other in a good mood (▲). When it comes to disciplining the children, some positive communication takes place but differing opinions and frustration (≈) mostly dominate. But when money comes up, serious miscommunication (≈) prevails and is beginning to build into distrust and resentment (▼).

A Closer Look at the Turbulent (≈) Spirit

A turbulent (≈) spirit is the weather front that both charges and changes the atmosphere of the home. It is generated by miscommunication. Robert and Elaine's confrontation about the credit card receipt for the hot-air balloon had changed the warm atmosphere into a frustrating, unsettled one. The mischievous IMP from the night before is alive again as they sit reading the morning paper:

They do not look at each other. Robert and Elaine are in the same room, but nothing seems to be going on between them. On closer inspection, however, there is a strange, powerful force—an invisible wall—preventing contact between them.

Elaine walks into the other room and notices clothes on the floor. "No one ever cleans up around here," she complains. The words hit Robert like a powerful shock wave. He immediately stiffens with the impact, clenching his teeth and throwing an angry look toward the other room. He freezes in that position, then lets out a heavy sigh and goes back to reading.

"This whole house is a mess," Elaine continues as she comes back into the room with Robert. But this time there is only the slightest stiffening of his neck and shoulder muscles as he receives the impact. He now seems totally indifferent and untouched by Elaine's presence.

Elaine sits back down, trying to get absorbed in the paper, but all she can feel is her frustration with Robert. Sure, there had been an argument, but now she wants some response from him. Anything, even a show of anger, would be better than the awful silence. It was as if she did not even exist for him.

Robert feels the upset in his stomach growing. *Why does everything seem to bother her?* he wonders. *When she gets into a mood like this, nothing I do seems right to her.* He then goes back to reading, trying to make the uncomfortable feeling inside go away.

The atmosphere is one of frustration and confusion, the unsettled feeling of a turbulent relationship. Both are upset by the actions of the other. Each person—each spirit—is sending out energy into the shared spirit. But it

28

is not reaching the other side; it is blocked from uniting. Both are left frustrated. The energy collects and the feelings are stuck, unable to reestablish contact.

It may appear as if the relationship is now without spirit. Actually, there is a powerful force now living in the shared spirit, that is, a turbulent ($\approx$) spirit collecting all that stuck energy.

The Critical Moment in the Relationship

When the atmosphere is inevitably changed by the frustration produced by a turbulent spirit, a critical moment is reached. At this point Robert and Elaine have two options. They can either *confront the differences openly* so that the turbulent ($\approx$) atmosphere can be reconciled into a good ($\blacktriangle$) spirit. Or they can *allow the frustration and hurt to stay blocked* in the middle of the relationship. This blocked frontal system will gradually stagnate to form bad ($\blacktriangledown$) weather in that area.

The Atmospheric Inversion

The natural inclination of a turbulent spirit is a downdraft into a bad spirit (Gen. 8:21; Eph. 4:18; Rom. 3:11–12). There is a force of evil that flows downward, seeking to preserve the bad mood, justifying further destruction of the relationship by nursing one's hurt feelings and by getting even. This force is brought to the space by our own sinful nature and by Satan, whose name comes from a word meaning "to obstruct." The devil uses our sins, which obstruct our relationship with God, to divide us against each other (Eph. 4:27). Satan uses disguise, deception, and pride to intensify the division (Rev. 12:9; 20:10). As the energy moves downward, the mood stagnates in the atmospheric inversion ($\blacktriangledown$) and becomes colder and harder as the "dividing wall of hostility" (Eph. 2:14) begins to build in the center of the shared space. The shared space cracks, and a turbulent spirit changes into an inverted spirit, a spirit turned inward. This inverted spirit is a "bad" spirit.

The Path of Inversion

The spirit of the relationship becomes unsettled when one person's feelings are hurt by the other. Often this spirit or mood develops through a misunderstanding in which the hurt was unintentional. Elaine again tried to make contact that morning, but her intention was misunderstood:

> Right before they both were ready to go to work, Elaine mentioned that it might cost too much to take the family up in a hot-air balloon. Robert responded defensively: "Why do you say that?" Elaine continued, "Well, you *have* spent quite a bit lately . . ." Robert could feel his throat tighten. He glared at Elaine for a second. Then he turned and walked out with a parting comment: "Yeah, I know . . . I can't be trusted!" And he slammed the door behind him in anger.

Elaine had not intended to hurt Robert's feelings. She was simply expressing a real concern that she had on her mind. She was open to discussing the issue, but her comments struck Robert as a criticism of him. At that moment he felt put down; he had been made smaller in Elaine's eyes. Immediately the balance shifted from Robert's perspective. So he angrily slammed the door to even things up.

Because Robert did not take Elaine's comment in the right spirit, the atmosphere changed inside his own spirit. Although Elaine did not intend it, Robert thought that she did not respect his ability to handle money. Robert felt a powerful force inside that pushed him toward *getting even*.

His feeling of being put down by Elaine produced anger. Now anger is a sign that a relationship—a shared spirit—has come to a fork in the road. It can lead toward better or worse things in the future. At this point, there is nothing wrong with Robert's anger. The anger resulted from a misperception and is actually a healthy energy. "In your anger do not sin" (Eph. 4:26). The anger itself is not sinful, but it can lead to sinful actions. This began to happen with Robert.

Robert's flow into the natural downdraft let his anger turn into sin by *directing the anger toward Elaine.* This began the downward spiral. Elaine felt that his angry response was putting her down. She knew that she did not deserve his anger, so her feelings were hurt. To her, the balance was upset, and she felt compelled to get even.

Directing her anger at Robert as he left, Elaine let her anger become sin. Therefore, they broke contact in anger. The anger stuck in the shared space between them. The turbulent ($\approx$) atmosphere began heading toward the downdraft ($\blacktriangledown$). Unresolved anger controlled the weather.

As long as Robert's anger is aimed *toward* Elaine, he *will get even.* It is impossible for anyone to leave the relationship out of balance. He actually has no choice if he stays angry at Elaine. He will find a way of cutting her down to size to even things up.

There are many ways of getting even. Let's see how Robert and Elaine dealt with their anger toward each other:

The rest of that morning, Robert thought about the scene, letting his anger ferment inside. Some of his anger was vented when he let himself think, *She's just like her mother. She always finds something to argue about.* At that moment Elaine became less important and special to him.

Elaine went to work and began talking to her friends about Robert's immature actions. She felt better laughing at his defensiveness and mildly ridiculing him to her friends. One of her friends said, "Sounds like he just hasn't grown up yet." Elaine nodded in agreement. "That's Robert!" she said.

Do Not Let the Sun Go Down on Your Anger

If the misunderstanding is not cleared up and the anger is held over, a mischievous IMP will remain between Robert and Elaine when they go to bed. Satan then has an opportunity. " 'In your anger do not sin': Do not let the sun go down while you are still angry, and do not give the devil a foothold" (Eph. 4:26–27). And if Satan gets a foothold, you can be sure that he will make the most of it.

The next day the subject will probably be dropped. The atmosphere may shift as Robert and Elaine interact in other areas of their relationship. But the damage done by this unresolved anger will not go away.

After the sun has gone down and anger has festered for a time, hurt feelings gradually change into hard feelings. "Upset," "hurt," "frustrated," "angry," "confused," and "turbulent" describe hurt feelings. But when the feelings harden, there is a critical change in attitude toward the other person—a critical change in spirit. Words that describe hard feelings are more like "bitter," "hateful," "disgusted," "resentful," and "evil" (Eph. 4:31).

At this point the anger has turned into sin. The turbulent spirit is now a bad spirit. The mischievous IMP ($\approx$) becomes a fiendish IMP ($\blacktriangledown$). This brings about a critical shift in *intent*. While the spirit was turbulent, the intention was to even up the relationship. The purpose was to say to the other person, "You hurt or belittled me!" This gives the other person the chance to acknowledge the hurt that was caused and your right to be angry. Then the anger will dissipate.

When the anger doesn't dissipate and hard feelings develop, a *deliberate attempt to hurt* the other person ensues. This intent to hurt is evil and becomes the basis of a "dividing wall of hostility" (2:14). Hard attitudes form within one's spirit and between two people. This "grieves the Holy Spirit" (4:30). These hardened attitudes breed adultery, deceit, slander, and hatred. This is what eventually will destroy the spirit of the family.

Why Is This a Natural Downdraft?

When one's feelings and pride are hurt, a natural process of justification takes place within a person. The person feels *absolutely justified* in getting even. As part of our sinful nature, this trait shows up early in life. Later on these same feelings may show up on bumper stickers: "Don't Get Mad. Get EVEN!"

No one has to teach a little child how to say, "He did it first!" or "Don't blame me; I had a right to do it!" These are ways of justifying our actions, and they show up any time our feelings have been hurt. It just seems obvious that we have a right to get even.

Well-intentioned friends will help push this natural downdraft (▼) along. When Elaine talked to her friends at the office, they comforted her by saying, "I don't blame you." They reinforced her right to stay angry at Robert.

God Creates the Updraft (▲)

A strong Scriptural statement aims at reconciling the differences before they turn into stagnant, hard feelings. "If you are offering your gift at the altar and there remember that your brother has something against you, leave your gift there in front of the altar. First go and be reconciled to your brother; then come and offer your gift. Settle matters quickly with your adversary who is taking you to court. Do it while you are still with him on the way" (Matt. 5:23–25). This is good advice.

It is easy to regard conflict and the frustration and confusion that follow as destructive to a relationship. But it is not. This view justifies a strategy of merely avoiding or walking away from conflict. But that is not a healthy strategy.

A healthy spirit between two people does not come from staying on good terms with one other. It comes from facing the differences that caused the conflict so that they can be reconciled into a deeper understanding. Each per-

33

son must remain an individual in—yet vitally concerned with—the relationship. That is what makes a healthy spirit. If one either always gives in or never gives in, there is no spark in the relationship. "Everyone will be salted with fire. Salt is good. . . . Have salt in yourselves, and be at peace with each other" (Mark 9:49–50).

A relationship purified by fire (Mal. 3:2) faces differences of opinion openly and honestly, keeping the salt but searching for new ways of understanding that will reconcile the differences. The atmosphere of a turbulent spirit may become the occasion when God Himself, the "purifier" foretold by Malachi, brings His creative energy to deepen the relationship.

The Path of Conversion

Anger can be the spark to get the fire of the relationship going again if directed appropriately. If it works to restore the relationship, it results in a turning toward one another—which can be called "conversion." The updraft occurs when the two spirits turn from their individual focus and are reunited.

The anger that comes from being hurt is not sinful at all. This is *clean* anger and is essential for the health of the relationship. This anger does create an initial confrontation in the relationship, temporarily unsettling it. But that's the only way to clear the air and recreate the updraft of two sharing rather than divided spirits.

But anger can and often does turn into sin. Anger of itself is not sin, but the inappropriate expression of anger against another person turns anger into sin. *Misdirected* anger blames the other person for the hurt feelings.

The unresolved hurt gradually changes the attitude toward the other person. The resulting resentment and bitterness now become the *dirty* anger that usually is expressed in a disguised form to hurt the other person.

Good anger is directed at the relationship so that the air can be cleared and the warmth of the good spirit can be restored. Examples of this *clean* or reuniting anger are "Hey, what you said didn't sit right with me. We need to talk this over!" or "I'm not sure what it was, but something just happened between us. We've got a problem that we need to deal with." This kind of anger invites the other person to join in and help clear things up. It is experienced as a determination to restore a good spirit. Then the atmosphere can shift in the upward direction.

This is hard to put into practice. When feelings are hurt, it seems that the other person has caused your distress. Anger naturally directs itself at the apparent cause of the problem—the other person. We often have said things like "How can you *say* that?" or "OK, then, have it *your* way! See if I care!" *Our inner nature wants to hold on to the bad feeling toward the other person.*

God's Spirit, working through His Word, helps change this attitude. For the anger to be directed at restoring the spirit between the two persons, values must shift. The downdraft (▼) of a bad spirit nurses hurt pride and pushes toward the destruction of the family unit. But God gives us the insight of His Word. He has taken decisive action, sending His Son to make peace with us and forgive us by taking our sin on Himself and dying for us when that was required. On the basis of His action, our style of dealing with one another can change. This renewal of values sets us free from our self-centeredness. "Do not conform any longer to the pattern of this world, but be transformed by the renewing of your mind" (Rom. 12:2).

God's Spirit helps us to value the spirit of the relationship above self: "Submit to one another out of reverence for Christ" (Eph. 5:21). In practice this means swallowing our pride for the sake of reconciliation. It means giving up our perceived right to get even for the sake of the family spirit. This is not natural. The Spirit helps convince us of the ultimate importance of this updraft (▲). A good family spirit is well worth the effort. Robert and Elaine made that extra effort the next evening:

The mood in the house was heavy. Robert and Elaine were still not talking to each other. The children felt it and stayed in their rooms. Elaine knew that what she and Robert were feeling was wrong. While she was talking to God about her frustration, things seemed to straighten out inside her head. She came out to the garage where Robert was working. "What are you doing?" she ventured, attempting to re-establish communication. But Robert wasn't ready to make contact, so he replied with a curt "Nothing!" and turned away from her. Feeling rejected, Elaine turned and went back into the house. Minutes later, Robert, uneasy over his response to Elaine, prayed for a change of heart. He went to find Elaine and asked, "Does this look about right?" But Elaine, still agitated, snapped, "Can't you tell?" With that Robert retreated again back into the garage. Finally, about a half hour later they were both open at the same time. Robert came back in and sat down, looking at Elaine. Elaine picked up his nonverbal signal and began, "I guess we need to talk about what happened this morning." Robert agreed, "Yeah, I think I took you wrong. I've been thinking it over. I'm beginning to think we need to talk more." "Yeah," Elaine agreed, "and I'm beginning to realize that you do not mean to hurt me when you walk away like that." A few minutes later, the children looked with pleasant surprise as their parents were sitting close together, laughing at a family situation comedy on TV.

Robert and Elaine stayed in there and, prompted by the Holy Spirit, struggled to shift the unsettled mood. They have a long way to go, but they are at last on the right road.

Remember this the next time you are upset and angry

with one of your family members and the spirit is broken between the two of you. Though you may not be able to do it right away, feel the upward (▲) tug and pull of the Holy Spirit toward putting the spirit of the family above your right to get even. Let this struggle for reconciliation become a part of the lifestyle of your family.

Chapter 2: Weather Watch Activities

1. Think of the last time your feelings were hurt or you felt put down. What is vivid about the situation? Can you remember the exact words or the look on the other person's face? Did you feel smaller, less important?

2. The natural internal reaction to hurt is anger. What did your anger feel like? Where did you feel it (chest, hands, eyes)? What impulse did you have? What did you really want to do or say at that moment? Don't ask us to print it!

3. When you felt put down, the relationship was no longer in balance. The anger is there to even things up. How did you get even in this situation? Did you

- do it internally by making that person less important to you?
- talk about that person to someone else?
- do something hurtful back to that person (angry look or critical words)?
- all of the above?
- more than all of the above?

4. Think back over the past few weeks and remember times when you were upset at work, home, or some other place. Which of your relationships seems to be the most turbulent?

5. Next look at situations when you have been put down. How did you usually even things out. Do you withdraw and get moody? Do you strike back? Do you talk to others about the situation? Do you go back over the sit-

uation in your mind again and again, thinking of ways to react?

6. Go back to the relationship that seems to be the most turbulent. Do you feel things building up between the two of you? Can you describe the IMPs being carried over from one encounter to the next?

7. Pick one of the situations that you have remembered and try a different strategy. Go back to that person and describe how the situation struck you. This is clean anger. That's hard, isn't it? But it's worth it!

8. Deliberately ask one of your family members how you have hurt him or her in the past week. Ask that person to talk it over with you. See if you can change an unsettled situation into a good spirit (▲).

9. The next time you feel belittled or put down, try something different. (a) Assume that you misunderstood something. (b) Express your hurt right away (before the sun goes down on your anger). (c) Work to clear up the misunderstanding, changing the atmosphere from unstable ($\approx$) to fair (▲).

10. Think of a relationship in which the feelings have gotten stagnant (▼). Trace how these feelings gradually developed over time. Can you see how the turbulent spirit ($\approx$) gradually changed into a bad spirit (▼)?

12. Think of your most important relationship. Draw a weather chart of your shared space like that given in this chapter. Divide the space into three important areas. Then put a "▲," "$\approx$," or "▼" into each of the areas to show what the atmosphere is usually like after that subject has come up.

13. Have the other person draw that shared space also and compare charts. Look at how similar the two of you draw the charts. That is why it is called a "shared space"— both of you feel the same forces in that space.

14. Then draw a picture of the space between you and other family members in the same fashion. Compare charts with these members of your family also.

Notes

1. Gestalt psychology suggests that for a healthy flow of energy in a relationship, the individual differences cannot be blocked but must have the freedom to be expressed. Also, the concept of "unfinished business" parallels the turbulent ($\approx$) IMPs. These must be confronted and worked through to unblock that area of the relationship. (See J. Fagan, *Gestalt Therapy Now* [New York: Harper and Row, 1970].)

2. Our culture has done a good job of advocating the rights of individuals. In the courtroom where the issue is the division of marital property, lawyers will go to any length to advocate the rights of the husband or of the wife. But is there anyone who advocates the rights of the marriage itself? Is there anyone to object when the question might further damage the relationship between the two? Scriptural insight places the highest value on service to others. This is much different from current cultural directives that stress the right to personal happiness.

3. The *Random House Dictionary* defines "imp" as (1) "a small demon"; (2) "a mischievous child"; and (3) as a verb associated with falconry, "to improve powers of flight." Thus the term "IMPs" carries the connotations of evil, of the uncertain actions and intentions of children, and of positive and helping support.

4. Both *Building a Christian Marriage* by Ron Brusius and *Christian Family Communications* by Julaine Kammrath (Concordia Publishing House) have several good exercises that teach a family how to turn a turbulent spirit into a good spirit or how to handle conflict creatively.

Before You Read Chapter 3

Have you . . .

. . . ever wished people were more like you?
Look at 1 Corinthians 12:4–11.
But God gave each of us different gifts. Some family members *paint pictures* as they talk. Call them *painters.* Some family members like to get right to the *point.* Call them *pointers.* And do they talk past each other!

. . . ever thought that differences are necessary?
Look at 1 Corinthians 12:12–20.
An eye and an ear sure experience the world differently! Painters seem to notice everything. Pointers are usually thinking about something else. And my, oh my, they are different!

. . . ever felt misunderstood?
Look at 1 Corinthians 12:21–26.
How can you feel deeply for another family member unless you really get to know how that person feels? Painters and pointers feel differently. Do you know which one you are?

Chapter 3

Turbulence: When Personalities Clash Like High- and Low-Pressure Systems

Robert was completely absorbed in the evening paper when Rose came in the room and asked Elaine, her mother, "Can I run over to Beth's for a while?" "No. You have homework to do," Elaine replied. "I've been working on my homework!" Rose answered back, her voice showing an edge of anger. "The answer is no, and that is final!" Elaine snapped back, upset at Rose's attitude. With that, Rose stomped out of the room and slammed the door. Elaine, obviously upset, looked at Robert. "Are you going to let her get by with that?" she shot at him. "With what?" Robert answered, puzzled at her reaction. "I don't believe you!" Elaine exploded. "You just sat there and let your daughter make me look like a fool." "But . . . but . . ." Robert replied defensively, "she was talking to you!" "OK, put it all on me like you always do," Elaine said with a note of bitterness in her voice. "Then you can come out as the good guy!" With that, Robert threw down the paper, got up and heaved a big sigh as he walked out of the room. As the door shut, Elaine wanted to scream with frustration.

A shift from a sunny, warm atmosphere to an unsettled, frustrating one is never welcome. But conflict is inevitable, healthy, and necessary for an exciting and vibrant relationship. The creative energy of the family unit arises out of the differences that each individual brings to the family. These differences are actually God's gifts to the family. "There are different kinds of gifts, but the same Spirit" (1 Cor. 12:4).

Differences bring about change and development in weather patterns. The clash of high- and low-pressure systems creates changes in weather. Differences are the minimum requirements for relationships. The gift of these differences cannot be overvalued (Rom. 12:6–8).

One of God's gifts is our personality. It directs our actions, guides how we deal with reality, and governs our whole style of communication. There are many ways of describing personalities. One way is to look at two types: the externalizer and the internalizer. For simplicity we will refer to them as *painters* (those who *paint* pictures when talking) and *pointers* (those who summarize things, stating only the *point*), respectively. Although few people are distinctly one or the other, you can probably tell which group you fall into.

Meet an Externalizer (A Painter)

Elaine Spring notices everything. She watches people's expressions closely, and quickly picks up the vibrations they send out. She is aware of her surroundings at all times and stays aware even when she is trying to concentrate. She is involved with a number of things at the same time.

Things that she must do stay in her mind until they get done. She tries to resolve things and remembers things from the past that have not been resolved. When she gets upset, she has absolute recall of past events that relate to her emotions and vividly expresses those feelings all at once.

She searches out other people, especially when she feels emotions stirring inside. She wants to share her feelings as soon as possible. When she talks, she goes into colorful detail. At times her conversation jumps around to different things, as if she were painting a portrait of her feelings. If she feels that she is being misunderstood, she becomes frustrated.

The worst emotion that she experiences is loneliness. She hurts when another person withdraws from her; she struggles to restore contact. At times she will deliberately start a conversation with a strong statement just to get a feeling across. She initiates things and is creative in thinking up new things to do.

Meet an Internalizer (A Pointer)

Robert Spring often has his mind on other things. He misses out on much of what is going on around him. Often he will not react to subtle emotional messages and hints sent out by another person. He concentrates on one thing at a time and can lose himself in the task; he may be oblivious to what is going on around him.

He can forget about a problem by putting it out of his mind so that he is not aware of it for a time. Often it appears that things do not bother him much. He does not like to bring up past hurts and often says, "It's not that big a deal. Let's just forget about it." When he gets upset, he would rather go off by himself and work things out inside his head. This lets him get things back into perspective. When he talks, he sticks to the point and uses as few words as possible. Much of the time his voice and facial expressions are controlled, giving only a hint of emotion. He does not like to repeat things. If he does not get his point across, he will shrug it off and say that it was not all that important anyway.

To him, the worst emotion is helplessness. He always wants to find a solution to the problem. He feels burdened or guilty if something is wrong.

Differences Are Energy

"When high and low clouds do not march together, there will be a change in the weather" (an old farmer's saying).

The differences between Elaine and her husband, Robert, like high- and low-pressure systems pushing against each other, produce energy for the spirit of their relationship. The basis for this energy is the endless fascination and attraction that these differences produce. A good relationship is built on learning to understand and appreciate the differences by viewing them as gifts from God (Rom. 12:6).

There is a vast difference in how people deal with their thoughts and feelings. An *externalizer* (painter) is aware of many things at once. An *internalizer* (pointer) focuses on one thing at a time. Their brains work differently, according to the way they process information. This difference can be, and often is, the source of recurring conflict and misunderstanding. (Compare the different personalities of Mary and Martha in Luke 10:39–40.)

Some Points of Difference

There are certain characteristics of each personality that we can describe. But keep in mind that these differing

45

characteristics are presented as extremes. Not all the items might apply to a given person. What is important is to note the areas where real differences exist between two family members.

Externalizer (Painter)	Internalizer (Pointer)
1. Will talk around the subject, giving different details—*paints a picture.*	1. Will *get right to the point,* summarizing things and giving generalizations.
2. The first thing a *painter* says is rarely the point but is the *first brush stroke* of the picture.	2. The first thing a *pointer* says *is usually the point* and all other things said will relate to that point.
3. Tends to *overstate* the emotional importance of a situation so it can get expressed.	3. Tends to *minimize* the emotional importance of a situation so it can be put into perspective.
4. Is usually a *good talker*—feels best when expressive.	4. Is usually a *good listener*—feels best when the other person is in a good mood.
5. *Cannot put things out of mind.* Anything unfinished is always somewhere in consciousness.	5. *Can put things out of mind.* It takes no effort to file things away and forget about them.
6. Will *continue to notice* other things when concentrating.	6. Will often *be oblivious of* other things when concentrating.
7. Will *divide concentration* among several things at once, devoting a percentage to each.	7. Will *devote complete attention* to one thing and then shift to something else.

8. *Notices things* like facial expressions and mood changes—is sensitive to subtle cues from others.
9. Will have a definite and *obvious emotional reaction* to a situation.
10. Is *comfortable feeling emotion* and needs to get emotional when something happens.

11. *Needs to express* emotions. Otherwise, things stay stirred up inside.
12. *Will try to make contact* with the other person when that person is upset—will try to get the other to talk.
13. When angry, has a *perfect memory for past hurts.*
14. Will see a potential problem and *try to deal with it* before it gets worse.
15. Will feel and express a *wide variety of emotions,* going from high to low in a short period of time, shifting moods easily.

8. *Does not notice such things* unless deliberately aware—is not as sensitive to subtle cues from others.
9. Will *first think about* the situation and then give an *analysis* of things.
10. *Emotion is unsettling* so tends to detach from the situation when something emotional happens.
11. Needs some space to be alone, to work out conflict and to *let things settle down.*
12. Will *tend to withdraw* from the other person when that person is upset—will leave the other alone.
13. When upset, *focuses all anger* on one thing.
14. Will tend to *overlook problems* so as to stay optimistic.
15. Will *stay calm in emotional expression,* not getting angry easily, but also slow to get out of a bad mood.

And They Attract Each Other!

There is quite a difference between these two personality types, especially in the way they handle emotion. The painter is more like a high-pressure system, reacting with high internal emotion to situations. The pointer is more like a low-presssure system, reacting with low internal emotion to situations. When each is upset, their reactions differ as a thunderstorm differs from a drizzle. The painter often gives strong, immediate reactions, while the pointer just gets moody.

A pointer is attracted to a painter because of the way painters, like thunderstorms, can stir things up, making them seem more alive and exciting. A painter is attracted to a pointer because pointers, like a drizzle, provide stability in the relationship.

But the thing that attracts pointers and painters to each other becomes most annoying when the relationship breaks down. Recall how annoyed Elaine, the painter, got at the lack of emotional reaction from Robert when Rose talked back. In turn, Robert, the pointer, resented Elaine's making such a big deal out of it.

How Pointers Deal with Conflict

When there is conflict, the pointer's natural defense is to subdue the aroused emotion. Strong emotion is hard to handle. Pointers cannot sort things out when emotions keep getting stirred up. That is why they need to withdraw. Once the turmoil settles down inside, they can think again. Inside pointers the emotion gets broken up into manageable sections.

The process of dealing with emotion can be pictured as someone using a large internal filing cabinet. When a strong emotion hits, it is immediately pushed down into an "office" where it is broken up and neatly filed into different drawers. When the time is right—often when the pointer is alone—pointers will pull open one drawer at a time, sort through it, and regain perspective. Only then is the pointer ready to deal with the conflict.

How Painters Deal with Conflict

The natural reaction of a painter to conflict is to seek out continued contact in order to keep the emotion flowing. Unresolved emotion is hard to handle. A painter cannot push it aside as the pointer must. Inside painters the emotion keeps stirring. This process is like a continuously revolving drum. The painter may try to push it down and forget about it, but the thoughts and feelings will pop right back up. The painter needs to resolve the conflict to stop the recycling process.

How Storms Develop

The painter is determined to face the issue immediately. The pointer is determined to let things settle down first. In this clash of high- and low-pressure systems, storms develop.

It is precisely the pointer's withdrawal from contact that the painter misunderstands. "If something is important to me," Elaine, the painter, reasons, "I won't put it out of my mind. And here, right after we try to discuss the issue and I am all stirred up, how can Robert turn over and go to sleep? He doesn't care!" And we have all the makings of mischievous IMPs ($\approx$) beginning to collect in the shared space.

Since painters react differently, they perceive withdrawal as either a lack of caring or an attempt to hide something. Neither is true. Pointers are just dealing with the conflict in their natural style. They care just as much and are just as interested in the relationship, but they must deal with the emotion differently.

In turn, pointers will think that painters are simply "going on and on" or "bringing up the subject again and again." They see this as a deliberate attempt to make them feel bad. "Why else would Elaine go on and on," Robert, the pointer, reasons, "when it is obvious that nothing can be done about it?" And we again see mischievous IMPs

($\approx$) collecting in the shared space.

A pointer misreads the need of the painter to resolve the issue. Pointers assume that painters are trying to rub it in or to make pointers feel guilty by bringing up the past. This is not true. Painters have no option. They must talk it through in order to put the matter to rest.

Thus turbulent ($\approx$) conditions develop around the issue in conflict. Pointers try to put the issue aside. Painters try to keep it front and center.

Like a storm brewing, the pressure mounts. The illusive mood particles (IMPs) become "Intensified Mood Particles." Unless something takes place to cause a breakthrough, the storm will either gather force and momentum or settle into stalled deadness ($\blacktriangledown$). So what can be done about it?

Learning to Communicate

Robert and Elaine began to realize how different they really were. It took a lot of practice, but each gradually began to learn new ways of understanding. The communication skills that Robert and Elaine developed may also help you resolve conflicts. Pay particular attention to the comments addressed to the type you most identify with.

For Pointers—When Listening

A true breakthrough for Robert occurred when he finally realized that Elaine was not trying to make him feel bad. She had to express the things that were on her mind. She had no choice. Her peace of mind depended on her being understood.

Robert then discovered that he was asking for trouble if he responded to Elaine with minimizing statements like "Oh, it's not that important. Don't let it bother you like that!" These comments reflected his way of keeping things in perspective, but for the painter, the effect was frustrating. It stopped her flow of expression. Her feelings would endlessly recycle with no way of resolving them. Robert learned that a far better response to the emotion of a painter was to encourage more expression with an invitation like "Oh really? That sounds important! Tell me more."

Robert still has to catch himself. He reminds himself constantly that the first thing Elaine has to say is not the point. It is natural for a pointer to react to the first statement by drawing conclusions, but this is just the first brush stroke of a picture that is going to be painted. This first statement is usually a bold, powerful stroke to make contact. It is not the point. After all, no one would look at the first brush stroke of an artist and conclude, "Well, if that's what this picture is all about, I don't see much hope for it."

As Elaine painted her picture, she seemed to skip all over the place, leaving Robert wondering what she was trying to say. Much of what she said seemed irrelevant to Robert, and he would find himself growing increasingly impatient, looking for the point. Often he would even stop listening. As a sensitive painter, Elaine would immediately notice that he was no longer tuned in. She then had to add even more emotional expression to gain his attention, reiterating the situation again and again in an attempt to get the picture across. It took awhile, but Robert finally was able to sit back and become fascinated with the picture being painted. As she felt his interest, Elaine could happily paint away.

Robert's biggest struggle was to overcome his inclination as a pointer to take Elaine's need to express her emotions as a personal attack and to become defensive. He gradually realized that words did not have the same meaning for painters as they do for pointers. For painters, words are not logical symbols or literal statements but expressive pictures. So when Elaine would say, "This is it! I'll never do such-and-such for you again! Ever!" she did not mean that she is literally never going to do it again. She was just expressing her hurt and frustration. Robert finally learned to focus on the emotional overtone rather than on Elaine's words.

At first, to his surprise, Robert had realized that he did not trust Elaine. How could she say "I never want to talk to you again" one moment and then five minutes later be chatting away? She must not mean what she says. So Robert had to learn that Elaine was actually quite trustworthy. Her statements reflected her feeling at the moment. In fact, Robert grew to see her quick, changing emotional reactions as a strength she brought to their relationship. As a pointer, he needed that sudden reaction since it might take him some time to decide how he felt about things.

As a pointer, Robert's immediate response to any problem was to look for quick solutions. This was not what Elaine needed from him. Robert had to burn into his brain that she needed an opportunity to work through her feelings. A quick solution from him would not help at all. She first wanted to be understood.

For Pointers—When Talking

Robert was startled to realize that Elaine did not listen to his words but watched closely for any nonverbal expression of emotion. He learned to amplify his feelings by deliberately putting more emotion into his voice in order to communicate better with Elaine. He was amazed to learn how flat most of his summarizing comments were to Elaine and also found that he often did not look at her when he talked. He gradually was able to make direct eye contact and to use his hands and body to give greater emotional expression.

To show Elaine that he was just as interested in their relationship as she was, Robert went from initiating 3 percent of their conversations to starting things 15 percent of the time. It was not natural, but he began to start talking before he had gotten everything into a neatly organized package.

After Robert expressed the short, summarized point, he realized that he could not stop there, even though he had said all that he needed to say. He learned to go on and add concrete details so that Elaine could paint a picture in her mind and understand what he was trying to say.

For Painters—When Listening

The most critical thing that painter Elaine learned was that pointer Robert was not capable of the same emotional expression that she was. This did not mean that he felt less deeply about things. Nor was he trying to hide things. Elaine had to learn a new way of listening so that Robert could share more easily. Elaine's natural inclination was to get in there and try to dig it out. She would ask, "What's wrong? You've been acting strange lately; do you feel okay?" This is what she would want Robert to say to her, but it only made him retreat. Instead, she learned to provide an emotionally safe space where he could gradually open up. Pointers often do not know what they feel until they start talking. Therefore they need a safe atmosphere where they can gradually unfold what is emotionally important to them.

Elaine had a tough time learning that the first thing Robert said was the point and that it represented all of his feelings put into one package. Normally she would look past that first sentence, waiting for a picture to be painted. No wonder she would complain, "You never tell me anything," to which Robert would respond, "What else can I say? I've told you everything!" *The challenge to painters is to learn how to unwrap the package.* Since pointers do not need to be emotionally expressive or to "get things off their chests," they will make a generalized statement and then stop. It will end there unless the painter works to unwrap the package.

Elaine then learned that to unpack the point, she had to focus on one word and ask for more detail. Think of the process as starting from the center (the point) and gradually unfolding all of the detail. The following are unfolding responses that Elaine learned to make to Robert's one-phrase description of what happened during the day. You might want to cover up the response and compare it with your natural inclination:

Robert's Statement	Unfolding Response
a. My day went pretty *good* overall.	a. Tell me what didn't go so *good* for you.
b. Well, I guess the *meeting* didn't go quite like I wanted.	b. What happened at the *meeting?*
c. It wasn't too bad, but Jim wasn't too *helpful.*	c. What did Jim do that wasn't *helpful?*
d. His *comments* just were not all that supportive.	d. Tell me one of his *comments.*
e. When he said, "I think we need to study this more," I was *puzzled.*	e. How was that *puzzling?*
f. He and I agreed before the meeting that we should go ahead with it. I did not know how to take his *delay tactic.*	f. How did his *delay tactic* leave you feeling?

g. I guess I am angry with him. He's done that before. He will act like my good buddy when we are there alone, but when others are around, he will see which way the wind is blowing and then will say what he thinks will get him the most points with the group. I've about had it with him!

Once Robert got warmed up, he gave Elaine all the detail she needed to paint her own picture of his day. It usually takes several good unfolding responses to reveal what is on the pointer's mind.

To her surprise, Elaine discovered that Robert's emotions react much like a skittish fawn—one quick move and they will be gone. So it was important that she learned to handle what was being said with care. Rather than judging, criticizing, or challenging, she assumed that she did not yet understand what Robert was saying and simply asked for more detail.

Elaine had to break her habit of asking how Robert felt about something. Instead, she learned to ask what he was *thinking*. Pointers usually are not in touch with feelings but live up in their heads—just as painters live more in their hearts. Elaine grew to realize that access to Robert's feelings came through the unfolding process.

Elaine was also surprised to realize that she did not trust Robert. He could be obviously upset with her and yet say "I love you." *He is not saying what he really feels,* she would often think to herself. It took some time, but she learned that he really was saying what he felt. His words summarized his overall feelings. Even though he may have been momentarily upset, when he checked out all of his circuits, he still loved her.

Elaine grew to appreciate Robert's balanced emotional expression. This, she realized, was the strength that he brought to the relationship. As a painter, she needed that balance to keep things in perspective.

For Painters—When Talking

It was hard for Elaine to remember that Robert had the tendency to listen closely to the first thing she said. If he sensed an emotional attack coming, he would immediately get defensive and withdraw. She learned to preface her picture with "Something is bothering me, and I need you to listen so that I can sort through it." Robert could then get the point and prepare himself to watch a picture being painted.

Elaine would normally get upset and come on

stronger when she felt Robert tuning out, retreating, or getting defensive. She grew to realize that this only caused him to retreat more. She learned to stop and explain once again that she was just painting a picture and not attacking. It was as simple as repeating the sentence "Something is still bothering me and I need you to listen so that I can sort through it." That worked like magic.

Elaine had to burn into her brain that Robert's worst feelings were guilt, pressure, and helplessness. If what she said aroused one of those feelings, he would automatically retreat. Elaine learned to avoid initiating his retreat by physically pointing at her chest and saying, "What happened left *me* upset, and I need to talk to you about it," rather than, "Just why did you do that stupid thing?"

Taking Things in the Right Spirit

Most problems in any relationship begin with misunderstandings. It takes work by both people involved to confront and work it out. *But first both must be aware that there is a misunderstanding and that the other person did not intend to hurt.* Then there can be a true appreciation of the different strengths each brings to the relationship (1 Cor. 12:12–26).

Robert and Elaine began to understand the vast difference in the way they communicated and in the way they handled situations. As they applied this understanding to their situations, they found that the energy of the turbulent atmosphere could be turned into a deeper understanding and appreciation of each other. This was the starting point for deeper growth in their relationship. As some of the misunderstanding (mischievous IMPs) began to clear out of their shared space, a good spirit was more in control of the atmosphere of their home. They could begin dealing with other issues that brought turbulence in their relationship.

Chapter 3: Weather Watch Activities

1. Write down five different gifts that God has given to each of your family members. What is the strength that each brings to the family? Use a separate sheet of paper for each list. Share the lists. If you do this in a group, focus on one person at a time and have each read the list of strengths for that person. Give the lists to each person when you are finished. As an alternative, do this on each person's birthday.

2. Read through the items of this chapter that distinguish an externalizer (painter) from an internalizer (pointer). Decide which family member would fit into each category. Have fun with the items!

3. Take this concept outside the family to your work or with your friends. See how well these distinctions fit. Listen to others talk and see if you can tell if they are painting a picture or sticking to the point.

4. Listen to a painter and a pointer communicate. See if you can identify how they miss each other.
   a. Notice that the pointer will take the first thing said and assume that it is the point.
   b. Notice that the painter will overlook the first thing said and try to pull out the details.
   c. Notice which one gets frustrated when the other one says, "Well, what is the point?"
   d. Notice which one gets frustrated when the other one says, "Well, what else happened?"

5. If you are an internalizer (pointer), practice listening to an externalizer (painter) with the suggestions of the chapter in mind.
   a. Remember that this person is painting a picture.
   b. The first statement is only the first brush stroke.
   c. Be fascinated with the colorful detail.
   d. Do not try to solve anything.
   e. Ask for more detail if you do not get the picture.
   6. If you are a painter, practice listening to a pointer

a. Remember this person is summarizing things into a point.
b. Focus on the first thing said. Remember the exact words.
c. Take one of these first words and say, "Tell me more about _____."
d. Make it safe for the person to talk. Do not let yourself react until you have unfolded the point.
e. Remember that it will take four or five unfolding responses to get to the details.

7. If you are a pointer, practice talking to a painter using the suggestions from this chapter.
a. Remember that the painter needs detail, so do not stop with the summarization.
b. Remember that the painter is tuned to your non-verbal expressions, so get some energy into your voice.

8. If you are a painter, practice talking to a pointer with the suggestions of this chapter in mind.
a. Remember that the pointer takes a cue from your first words, so start with "I'm going to paint you a picture, so just settle back and watch."
b. Remember that the pointer easily becomes defensive, so paint your picture on the wall, not in the listener's face.

9. If you are a pointer, burn the following into your brain and refer to it often when dealing with a painter:

A painter must express things in order to let them go; therefore, the painter is not bringing something up to make you feel bad but is simply trying to express something for you to understand.

10. If you are a painter, burn the following in your brain and refer to it often when dealing with a pointer:

A pointer cannot think when too much emotion gets stirred up; therefore, the pointer is not withdrawing because he or she does not care but is simply trying to let things settle down inside.

Notes

1. The distinction between internalizer (pointer) and externalizer (painter) follows the concept of personality types made popular by the Myers-Briggs Type Inventory (I. Myers, *Introduction to Type* [Palo Alto, Calif.: Consulting Psychologists Press, Inc., 1980]). The distinction presented in this chapter, however, is novel. It is quite different from the extrovert/introvert distinction of Myers-Briggs. In fact, an internalizer may actually be an extrovert in that he or she has no trouble speaking out.

2. In my research on this personality distinction, I have found that about 70 percent of the externalizers are women and about 70 percent of the internalizers are men. Perhaps the culture influences this percentage by allowing women greater freedom of emotional expression than men.

3. The miscommunication between the externalizer and the internalizer can be called an "attribution error" from attribution theory in social psychology (M. Ross and G. Fletcher, "Attribution and Social Perception," in G. Lindzey and E. Aronson, eds., *Handbook of Social Psychology* [New York: Random House, 1985]). Such an error suggests that something was taken in a way in which it was not meant (in the wrong spirit).

Before You Read Chapter 4

Have you . . .

. . . ever felt strongly about someone?
Read Psalm 42:1–2 and 1 Samuel 18:1.
How deep do your family bonds go? How about God's family? Remember a time of special closeness. Does it still bring tears to your eyes? I hope so!

. . . ever been absorbed by your attraction to a special person?
Read Mark 10:6–9.
God made men and women to be different. And the difference is an endless source of fascination . . . and frustration!

. . . ever seen a man strut around? How about the vengeance of a woman scorned?
Look at Ephesians 5:21–33.
Why the different instructions? Could the deepest need of the male be respect? Could the deepest need of the female be love?

. . . ever felt that a parent-child conflict could blow the roof off your house?
Look at Ephesians 6:1–4.
These emotions are also powerful. What is your child really looking for?

Chapter 4

Deeper Turbulence: The Clash of Powerful Sexual and Parental Emotions

The mood was good and romantic. It was an escape weekend for Robert and Elaine. They chatted about many things on their way to the beach. They found that they could enjoy each other as much as when they were dating. They lingered over dinner and followed that by an evening walk along the beach. Their discussion ranged over their concerns and dreams for their children and the renewed closeness of the family. Everything seemed perfect as they walked back to their motel room. The depth of closeness was back again.

God placed the bonding emotions deep within the soul. These emotions give us the capacity to love and to form strong family connections. Because these emotions are placed within the soul, we yearn to fulfill them.

An example of the depth and yearning of these emotions lies in a familiar Biblical friendship: "When he had finished speaking to Saul, the soul of Jonathan was knit to the soul of David, and Jonathan loved him as his own soul" (1 Sam. 18:1 RSV). The fulfillment of the yearning of the soul brings happiness to our lives. "A longing fulfilled is sweet to the soul" (Prov. 13:19).

These are the same deep emotions that yearn for God

and bond with Christ as part of His family. "As the deer pants for streams of water, so my soul pants for you, O God" (Ps. 42:1). "My soul clings to you; your right hand upholds me" (63:8).

We yearn for closeness. These are the deep, bonding emotions. Whenever these emotions are stirred, our moods and the atmosphere of the home can be abruptly changed.

These are familiar emotions, the "family" emotions that form the bonds between family members. The "familiar" emotions exist within the bonds, where the family unit is "joined and held together." Within the shared space, these powerful emotions produce deep energy for the family when set in motion by close contact. With this energy free to be expressed, the relationship can soar to great heights in the updraft (▲) of a good spirit. Or if these deep emotions get hurt, watch out for extreme turbulence (≈)!

One of these bonding emotions is the basis for sexual attraction. These emotions are part of the power of God's creation—His plan from the beginning to create us as man and woman. Though human sinfulness has often misused this gift, these emotions have roots deep within the male and female and represent the potential energy for the marriage relationship:

> "At the beginning of creation God 'made them male and female.' For this reason a man will leave his father and mother and be united to his wife, and the two will become one flesh. So they are no longer two, but one. Therefore what God has joined together, let man not separate." (Mark 10:6–9).

The unity that results from the bonding of the sexual emotions is mysteriously powerful. For Christian couples, it is so strong and mysterious that when properly grounded on God's love for us, it is an earthly echo of Christ's relationship with the church. " 'For this reason a man will leave his father and mother and be united to his wife, and the two will become one flesh.' This is a profound mystery—but I am talking about Christ and the church" (Eph. 5:31–32).

With the strong energy of these sexual emotions, marriage need never become boring. This energy that God created in the soul lasts a lifetime, ever mysterious and intricate. But with the mystery comes misunderstanding and turbulence ($\approx$)—and a lifetime of searching for deeper understanding.

A High School Romance

Their eyes first met across the lunchroom on the second day of the school year. They were both freshmen and a little anxious about a new school, but when their eyes met, something happened to change the mood. They looked at each other a full four seconds and then looked away. But many times during that lunch period, they found each other's eyes again.

It took Mike several weeks to get up the courage to talk to her. He was finally prompted to do so when his friend gave him the word that she liked him. Little did he know that Rose had passed that word along so that he would catch the signal.

They started meeting each other at the lunchroom and talking during breaks between classes. Soon they were inseparable and enjoyed every minute together.

But then a strange tension arose. Mike's buddies started teasing him about "being led around by the nose" by a girl that really "had her hooks in him." He felt a strange force changing the weather inside him. He felt the need to prove that he was in control of the situation. So the next day he deliberately avoided Rose between classes and hurriedly sat with his buddies during lunch.

His behavior took Rose by surprise. She felt like a fool after she walked up to him during the first break, only to be completely ignored while Mike joked with some of the guys. Her friends immediately noticed the change in behavior and wondered if Mike wasn't dumping her for someone else.

Rose felt a strange force well up inside as she looked across the dining hall that day. She felt betrayed and uncertain. The atmosphere had mysteriously changed between them.

How Males and Females Are Truly Different

The emotional differences between males and females are closely connected with the physical aspects of sexuality. The body of a woman is designed to receive a man into herself. In the same way, she gives the depth of herself emotionally by opening herself, allowing a man to enter into her psyche and into her heart. Her greatest gift is to open herself to receive. True opening means being unprotected—being vulnerable. Consequently, her deepest fear is to be intruded on or used as an object of male pleasure. It is important for the male to treat this openness respectfully and to cherish it as a precious gift. The deepest need of the female is to be loved and cherished.

Just as the body of a man is designed to give a part of himself, so he has a strong desire to provide and to take care of the family. Perhaps we can best understand where male vulnerability lies by taking a look at what makes a man psychologically impotent, unable to give of himself. His deepest fear is to be controlled. It is most damaging to the male to feel the loss of freedom to make decisions. Masculinity is intertwined with accomplishment. It is important for the female to treat this strength with respect and to regard it as a gift to her.

God created the difference between male and female (Gen. 1:27) and the difference is attractive in an ever-refreshing way. But the difference is also the source of endless misunderstanding and hurt feelings.

The Sexual Relationship

Sexual intimacy is an intricate part of the husband-wife relationship and is an important extension of their communication. Touch and affection are the powerful mood-changing areas of the marriage. In the area of sexual intimacy, feelings become most sensitive, and critical misunderstandings occur.

> Robert was hurt and angry. He looked forward to the weekend with Elaine away from the children. But once they were in the motel, Elaine seemed to resent his advances. He didn't understand. He could only assume that she was punishing him for something.
>
> Elaine was hurt and angry. She also anticipated being away with Robert. But once they were in the motel, Robert seemed to ignore her feelings and wanted to jump right in bed. She did not understand. She was surprised by his aggressiveness. His strong sexual demands made her wonder if his previous tenderness was truly genuine.

Both Robert and Elaine have the same yearning for intimacy. But they achieve this intimacy quite differently. For Robert, sex is a means to intimacy or closeness; that is, sexual contact helps bring about intimacy. On the other hand, Elaine expresses intimacy through sex; that is, sexual contact is intimacy. So for the man, sexual contact *leads to* intimacy; for the woman, sexual contact *expresses* intimacy.

This emotional difference usually makes Robert the sexual aggressor. His yearning to get closer to Elaine arouses sexual impulses in him. When he senses rejection, he perceives Elaine's behavior as deliberately holding back affection in order to control him. He feels manipulated. His masculinity is at stake.

Elaine tends to look for nonsexual contact first in order to gain closeness. The closer she feels to Robert, the more sexually involved she becomes. If there is no emotional closeness, Elaine will perceive sexual advances as an intrusion. Almost automatically she will withdraw in order to protect her vulnerability.

The Threatened Male and Female

When Robert does not get the respect he needs and his maleness is threatened, he will instinctively try to protect himself by showing that he is in control. Instead of regarding her femininity with respect and love, he will either treat her coldly or forcefully demand affection. In this way he hurts Elaine where she is most vulnerable. Often this is done by showing an increasing disrespect for Elaine's body. He avoids complimenting her and lets her know that other women are attractive. Occasionally he cuts at her with "Well, it looks like you have put on a few pounds lately." You can imagine how feminine that makes Elaine feel!

When Elaine feels herself attacked by Robert, she instinctively protects herself by diminishing his power. She keeps his actions from hurting by belittling him. On several occasions she said cuttingly, "Why don't you grow up?" This certainly doesn't enhance Robert's masculinity.

It is easy to see the beginning of a continuous cycle: Robert and Elaine hurting each other in an attempt to protect their own vulnerability. The mischievous IMPs ($\approx$) follow the natural downward path and develop into fiendish IMPs ($\blacktriangledown$). A bad mood then sets in, sometimes for days, pulling the whole household into its downdraft ($\blacktriangledown$).

Robert and Elaine break the cycle when they realize that they do not intend to hurt one another. Each has reacted in a natural way to protect a threatened sense of self. The following directives of Scripture help them realize how to handle the differences in their emotional reactions.

After the basic directive to "submit to one another" (Eph. 5:21)—that is, to put the spirit of the relationship above self—St. Paul uses the example of the love between Jesus Christ and His church as a source for directives to husbands and wives.

For Males

"Husbands, love your wives" (v. 25) is the directive given specifically to men. Their role is to love and care for (v. 29) their wives.

When Robert's masculinity is hurt, he responds to Elaine as if she were cold and hard. He becomes insensitive to Elaine's basic need. This natural reaction only further damages their shared spirit. So St. Paul could in effect be saying to Robert, "For the sake of the spirit of your marriage, always regard your wife as precious and special to you, for then she will be able to show respect for you."

For Females

"Wives, submit to your husbands" (v. 22) is the directive given specifically to women. "Submit to" can also be translated "willingly show respect for." (See V. 33.) A respected husband will not feel the need to intrude on his wife's vulnerability but will protect and cherish her.

When her femininity is hurt, Elaine immediately shows a loss of respect for Robert, belittling him in some way. This natural reaction only further damages their shared spirit. St. Paul could in effect be saying to Elaine, "For the sake of the spirit of your marriage, always show respect for your husband, for then he can continue to respond in love to you."

Robert and Elaine had to make a conscious effort to resist their natural inclinations for the sake of their shared spirit. The next time the turbulent spirit showed up in the sexual area, they did not direct their energy inward to protect themselves. This time they stayed together and struggled to understand each other more deeply.

The escape weekend seemed doomed to failure for Robert and Elaine once the weather shifted in the motel room. Robert heaved a big sigh and turned on the TV. Elaine saw the old wall go up and felt like screaming again. The atmosphere was in a definite downdraft (▼) for the next half-hour. Elaine had tried a few comments, but Robert was not in the mood. Then Robert stood up, turned off the TV, and asked Elaine to go for a walk on the beach again. They walked in silence for awhile until Elaine ventured, "What happened to our evening?" Robert responded, "I don't know. I guess we need to talk about it. It felt like you changed on me when I pulled you down on the bed. The mood was good up until then." Elaine agreed, "Yes, it was good, but it felt like you changed when you suddenly pulled me down. I felt like you were attacking me." For the rest of the walk they talked about the sensitive sexual feelings that changed everything so quickly. They talked about things they had never discussed before. As they went back into the motel room, the good atmosphere was back and the updraft (▲) of the good spirit was quite evident. They held each other close, amazed at the change that had taken place.

The Parent-Child Relationship

Another set of relationships within the family unit contains an immense amount of energy—the bonding emotions between parent and child. Embedded within these feelings are issues of authority and acceptance.

Dawn had not been in a good mood that

morning. Her mother was getting upset with her attitude. Elaine asked for the third time that Dawn pick up her clothes. Dawn pretended that she did not hear anything. Elaine reached down, grabbed Dawn by the shoulders, and demanded, "Well are you going to do it or not, young lady?" Dawn hesitated a minute, and then with defiance in her eyes out came "No!" With that, Elaine marched Dawn straight to her room and ordered, "You will stay in this room until everything is picked up." As the door closed, Dawn just stood there looking at the clothes.

Parents have a God-given authority to instruct and train their children. "Teach them to your children and to their children after them" (Deut. 4:9). With this authority comes a deep need within the parent for honor and respect. "Children, obey your parents in the Lord, for this is right. 'Honor your father and mother'—which is the first commandment with a promise—'that it may go well with you and that you may enjoy a long life on the earth' " (Eph. 6:1–3).

Parents fear the loss of authority over their children. Parents can neither tolerate being made fun of nor allow a blatant show of disrespect. Such challenges will cause a parent to react harshly in order to regain the rightful position within this relationship.

The child deeply needs parental approval and praise. The child's basic feeling of worth comes from the regard of the parent for the child. The child hungers for the look, touch, or word that signals parental pride. The spirit of the child can only grow and develop in such an atmosphere of acceptance and approval. God created the child in such a way that a loving touch from the parent starts the spark of the child's spirit.

The child's fear is the loss of that approval—rejection or inability to live up to the expectations of the parent: "Fathers, do not exasperate your children; instead, bring them up in the training and instruction of the Lord" (v. 4). "Fathers, do not embitter your children, or they will become discouraged" (Col. 3:21). Children are doomed to self-doubt and internal struggles of worth. These embittered and discouraged children must embark on a lonely and lifelong journey, searching for a substitute for parental approval and love—sometimes in terribly destructive ways.

The Critical Misunderstanding

The parent will often misinterpret the child's quest for self-expression as a questioning of authority and will react in a way that will discourage the child. Children will often misinterpret a parental command as putting down their worth and will react in a way that will make the parents feel disrespect.

The result is damage on both sides and attempts to balance the relationship by more forceful expressions. More and more mischievous IMPs ($\approx$) begin to build up in the shared space. This then becomes a vicious cycle— a turbulent spirit ($\approx$) that over the years will get caught in the downdraft ($\blacktriangledown$) of a bad spirit, resulting in deep bitterness or hatred. Robert and his son were in that downdraft:

> Sonny was in a good mood. He had just gotten home from high school and was thinking back over the good conversation he had with a special girl. He did not even hear his father asking him to help carry in the groceries. The next thing he heard was an angry question, "Didn't you feel like getting up off your bed?" Feeling resentment from past accusations of laziness, Sonny growled back, "Are you saying that I don't do anything around here? Sometimes I don't believe you see very good!" With that, a cold knot hit the father's stomach. He slammed

the door to the room as he snapped bitterly, "I am sick and tired of you!" That set the atmosphere of the house for the evening.

A whole history of miscommunication was expressed in that brief moment. A stagnant atmosphere (▼) was setting in. The mood could change now with the slightest misunderstanding. Yet Sonny still felt a deep yearning for his father's pride, and Robert still sought his son's respect.

The Power of Touch

Touch can break through the mood like nothing else. A touch of acceptance or respect calms the fears and restores the relationship. Children yearn for that loving touch. A touch of forgiveness can restore a child's spirit.

Robert happened to be sitting next to his son in church. It was easy to see the tension between them as Sonny sat as far away as possible. Just then the words of the Gospel were read:

"The younger son . . . squandered his wealth in wild living. . . . So he went and hired himself out to a citizen of that country, who sent him to his fields to feed pigs. . . . When he came to his senses, he said, '. . . I will set out and go back to my father and say to him: Father, I have sinned against heaven and against you. . . .' While he was still a long way off, his father saw him and was filled with compassion for him; he ran to his son, threw his arms around him and kissed him" (Luke 15:13–20).

With the last sentence still ringing in his mind, Robert felt a strong need for reconciliation well up in him. He reached over and gently tugged on his son's shoulder. Then he whispered, "I'm sorry for what I said to you last night." Sonny hesitated a moment and then gave his father a subtle smile of understanding. Their eyes met and the old warmth and love passed between them once more. The good spirit was back!

Chapter 4: Weather Watch Activities

1. Remember the touch of a special person—grandparent, parent, or friend. Notice that you can still feel the touch. Anytime something is vivid in memory, deep emotions are involved.

2. Remember with your spouse or other family member special moments of touch and intimacy. As you express these to each other, feel the deep emotions that are still in these shared memories.

3. Do a touch history of yourself. Think of how often you were touched as a child and how often you are touched now. Notice how touch affects your own mood. Also notice how touch differs in each of your relationships.

4. Do a touch history of your family. Have there been any changes in how often your family members touch each other? Notice how touch affects and is affected by the mood of the house.

5. Establish minimum daily touch requirements for the health of your family. For the next week, each time you encounter a family member, touch each other. Hug or shake hands when you come home. Touch when you are watching TV together. Wrestle playfully with each other. Be sure to tickle someone—but not too hard and not too much!

6. Think of the times when you felt most like a man or a woman. Then think of the times when you felt least like a man or a woman. Share these times, if you wish, and talk deeply about what it means to be a male or a female.

7. Think back and try to come up with any messages you got from your parents about sex. Were they good

ones? Do you still feel the effects of those messages? Share this, if you wish.

8. Think of the sexual messages and values you want to pass on to your children. Talk these over with your spouse, if you wish. When you are clear and in agreement, bring the children in on the discussion so that these powerful messages are spoken and out in the open.

9. Notice how sensitive the mood is when it comes to sexual intimacy. Think of a time when the weather shifted quickly in this area. What went through your mind as the mood shifted? These are deep emotions.

10. Think of your dreams or ideal image of intimacy. Describe a picture that expresses your ideal or perfect image of closeness and intimacy, such as sitting in front of a fire or walking hand in hand on the beach at sunset. What is the mood? What would you talk about?

11. Search your memory. When did you feel that your parents were really proud of you. Then think of a time when you felt their disappointment. Does the emotion of both of those events still remain? Is there something you should have told them but didn't?

12. Can you vividly remember when you felt closest to each of your children. What made you the angriest with them?

13. What are some of your dreams for your children? What do you yearn for as you think of their lives?

Notes

1. The main purpose of the sexual emotions is not personal pleasure or recreation as the culture advocates. These emotions bond the family together. Thus any misuse of these emotions through promiscuity or infidelity damages the bonds of the family, weakening the family ties.

2. In recent years our society has focused considerable attention on equal rights for women. There is no question that this is an important development with both positive and negative results. Part of this emphasis, however, in-

volves a tendency to see males and females as being alike. This viewpoint can diminish what each uniquely brings to the relationship. After all, God created them male and female.

3. The concept that a child's spirit needs to be touched by the loving spirit of the parent before the child's self-image can develop feelings of worth and adequacy is similar to Karen Horney's concept of family warmth (K. Horney, *Neurosis and Human Growth* [New York: Norton, 1950]). If children are not affirmed (are "discouraged" in Scriptural terms), they spend the rest of their lives searching for the affirmation that comes from family warmth, sometimes in destructive ways.

Before You Read Chapter 5

Have you . . .

. . . discovered any sensitive topics around your home?
Look at Genesis 4:2–8.
Something sensitive happened between Cain and his
brother! Call this a "critical twist" or call it a demon—
it was in control.

. . . noticed problems in other members of your family?
Look at Matthew 7:1–5.
What about yourself? Maybe you are just sensitive in
that area. Remember any bad feeling you often had
when growing up? Remember having that feeling yesterday? See what I mean?

. . . ever faced a *deadly* mood around your house?
Read Ephesians 2:14–18.
Do you feel the "dividing wall of hostility"? Where is
that wall in your family? How about making a weather
prediction when the sensitive subject comes up between those two people?
SEVERE THUNDERSTORM WARNING!

. . . ever been possessed by an evil spirit?
Read Ephesians 4:30–31.
Well, have you ever *wanted* to hurt someone? Ever
wished evil on someone? I bet you have!

Chapter 5

Critical Turbulence: The Power of Different Backgrounds Clashing

Starting a family means taking two totally different histories and welding them together. Even with two fairly healthy spirits, there are many places where the two just do not want to fuse. Add to this the problems or baggage that people always carry with them. These are the unresolved conflicts of the past that each person carries as "mood particles" (IMPs) in his or her spirit. Throw it all together and out comes the critical turbulence—the area of atmospheric instability.

All new relationships are influenced by the experiences of previous relationships. We each bring both strengths and problems within our own spirit (IMPs) from the past into any present relationship.

Remember the Spring family. Many of Robert and Elaine's storms obviously developed around money. Planning a family outing in a hot-air balloon turned into a series of arguments over money. Let's take a look at how this critical turbulence developed:

> Robert was raised in a poor family and re-membered going to school with hand-me-down clothes that would not fit. Having been the brunt of jokes by his peers, he was embarrassed by the way he looked and by his lack of money to buy what he needed. He vowed that he would always have money in his pocket when he was old enough to work.

Elaine's father seemed to have no concern for money and would buy on impulse. Her mother was the one who saved and tried to be careful with money, only to be frustrated by Daddy's careless spending. Elaine felt her mother's hurt and frustration when Daddy would come home with another new "toy." Daddy did most of his buying after he had been drinking. Elaine gradually lost all respect for him.

During the first years of marriage, Robert and Elaine's weather chart looked like this:

Weather Chart between Robert and Elaine

family time	discipline	money
▲ ▲ ▲	▲ ▲	
▲ ▲	▲	
▲	≈ ≈ ≈	≈ ≈ ≈
	≈ ≈	≈ ≈
		▼ ▼ ▼
		▼ ▼

Unresolved turbulence (≈) swirls in the area having to do with disciplining the children. But it is easy to predict that money will be the most dangerous and unstable area in their relationship. You can see its downdraft (▼) already forming. The critical clashes that occurred in their communication centered around money. In fact, 70 percent of their arguments started over money. Elaine repeatedly questioned Robert about every penny he spent. Knowing the baggage she carried from her childhood, we can easily understand why she reacted as she did. Elaine felt intense anxiety over bills getting paid.

But Robert *misunderstood* (≈) her motives. Elaine seemed to be trying to return him to his childhood days of poverty. So he rebelled. To have some spending money and to avoid hassling with Elaine, he wrote checks that Elaine knew nothing about.

When Elaine found out what Robert was doing, she *misunderstood* (≈) his inner struggle. She felt that, just like her father, Robert could not be trusted, so she tightened the financial reins. He reacted by finding ways to hide money to ensure that he would have some to spend. The cycle of hurt and bad feelings spiraled between the two, filling the shared space with a more powerful downdraft (▼). After 16 years of marriage, the chart of their relationship looked like this:

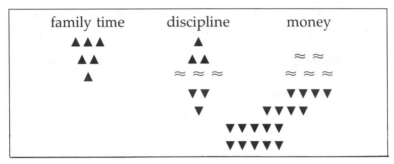

In spite of this deep trouble, Robert and Elaine could still make positive contact during family time. But the conversation could not get too deep. They could, for example, talk about what their daughter had done during the day (first cluster on the left). They were all right as long as the conversation did not deepen and sink into the downdraft (▼) that was spreading from the bad spirit in the area of money to other areas. But even though they were careful, talk about their daughter could lead to the subject of money:

"Didn't Dawn look pretty today?" Elaine began. Robert agreed and added, "She looked nice in that dress." Elaine responded with a slight edge in her voice: "It would be nice to be able to buy her more nice things." Robert caught the edge and countered with "Well, why don't we?" With that Elaine said coldly, "You know very well why we can't . . ." For the moment their eyes met, and hostility, resentment, and disgust were aroused in the shared space. They got caught in the downdraft (▼) of the bad spirit, and the mood shifted quickly.

A Deeper Look at Individual Backgrounds

We have seen how the history of any relationship is made up of the IMPs reflected in its spirit. In the same way, the spirit of each person reflects that individual's history of relationships. A bad relationship in the past is carried over into a new relationship. The fiendish IMP (▼) seems to be inhaled from the bad shared space, making an unstable area within the person's own spirt. The place in a new relationship where two unstable areas come together becomes the breeding ground for misunderstanding (≈) and eventually bad feelings (▼). Like the air masses that produce tornados, this is the critical turbulence in the relationship.

Awareness of these mood particles remaining in the spirits of two individuals can provide a *weather forecast.* Comparing the two individual histories can show areas of compatibility, understanding, and warmth. Such comparison can also show areas where unsettled and potential bad weather might be expected. Take a look at the feelings that Elaine's sister Alice and her boyfriend, Dan, carry over from before they met each other:

Held-Over Feelings (IMPs) from Dan's Background

friends	mother	work	play
	▲▲	▲	▲▲
	▲▲▲	▲▲	▲▲▲
▲▲	▲▲▲▲	▲▲▲	▲▲▲▲
≈ ≈ ≈ ≈	≈ ≈ ≈ ≈	≈ ≈	≈ ≈
≈ ≈	≈ ≈ ≈ ≈ ≈		
▼▼	▼▼▼		
	▼▼▼		
	▼▼		

81

Dan had other unsettled areas, but the most powerful set of emotions had to do with his mother.

Dan had never broken away from his mother. It was easy for her to continue to make him feel guilty and obligated to her. He was an only child, and his mother had raised him by herself, devoting all her energy to him. She saw Alice as a threat and treated her as such, calling Dan often at work to keep in contact with him. Dan did not see anything wrong with his love for his mother and couldn't understand why Alice had such a problem getting along with her. He assumed that all this would change when they got married.

Feelings Carried Over from Alice's Background

father	mother	school	piano
▲▲			▲▲
▲▲▲		▲	▲▲▲
▲▲▲		▲▲	▲▲▲
≈ ≈	≈ ≈ ≈ ≈	≈ ≈ ≈	
	≈ ≈ ≈	≈ ≈ ≈	
	▼ ≈ ▼	≈ ≈	
	▼▼▼		
	▼▼▼▼		
	▼▼▼		

Alice, on the other hand, was raised with a mother who was jealous of her closeness with her father. She was "Daddy's girl" and experienced negative reactions from her mother anytime she and her daddy did something special together. She was hurt repeatedly when Daddy would not stand up to Mother for her. Alice could not see that there was anything wrong about her negative reactions that resulted from Dan's not standing up to his mother for her, and which she directed toward Dan. She assumed that he had the problem and thought that he would finally break away from mother when they got married.

Knowing the backgrounds, we can predict the weather. Given the two charts, atmospheric instability over "mother" is predictable. In this area, their held-over feelings clashed.

Such instabilities carried over from the past are invisible until a new relationship is actually formed. What the individual carries over will surface only as the relationship develops enough depth to penetrate the insulation of each person's emotional history. Dan and Alice had had no idea what bad weather was in store for their relationship when they began dating.

Dan and Alice had met while playing tennis and began seeing each other often after that. Though Dan lived alone, Alice thought it a little odd that he would eat virtually every dinner at his mother's house. She also discovered that his mother called his office several times a day. Since Alice was raised to be independent, she thought that Dan needed to break away. She made this observation many times, and Dan would not talk about it. He thought that she was just down on his mother.

As they dated, Dan and Alice had built a good relationship. A generally good atmosphere prevailed as they enjoyed working, playing, and saving money together. Arguments over Dan's mother and some conflict over work priorities were the only areas that held the power to shift the mood to a turbulent ($\approx$) state.

The following weather chart details the IMPs that collected over two years of dating in Dan and Alice's shared space. It is already easy to observe where the frontal systems were beginning to build.

The Shared Space between Dan and Alice

money	relatives	work	sports
▲ ▲			▲ ▲ ▲
▲ ▲ ▲		▲ ▲	▲ ▲ ▲
▲ ▲ ▲ ▲ ▲	▲ ▲	▲ ▲ ▲	▲ ▲ ▲
	≈ ≈ ≈	≈ ≈	▲ ▲ ▲
	≈ ≈ ≈ ≈	≈	
	≈ ≈ ≈		
	▼ ▼ ▼		
	▼ ▼		

The first cluster on the left involves the area of "money." This cluster has a good history. They even bought a piggy bank and saved dimes in it for their honeymoon.

The second cluster involves the area of "relatives." The numerous unresolved conflicts (≈) and the apparent downdraft of bad feelings (▼) show bad weather brewing in this area. A short call from Dan's mother could really stir things up.

The third cluster involves the area of "work." There is positive sharing but some misunderstanding.

The fourth cluster involves the area of "sports." A good part of their relationship was getting out and playing tennis together. They could have fun kidding around with each other while they played.

The Weather Forecast

A bad spirit (▼) is the downward force that distorts

anything that passes between two people. It acts like a demonic force in that shared space, taking anything that is communicated and twisting it in a destructive manner. The devil himself takes the friction between two sinful people and creates a barrier of anger, irritation, and misunderstanding. If a bad spirit is present, the conversation can go nowhere; there is no way to resolve an issue because nothing will be taken in the right spirit.

As the bad spirit (▼) pulls the mood down, it transforms the individual spirits of the two people. In the presence of a bad spirit, they are both capable of doing things they never thought they would do; each one might actually intend to hurt the other! The bad spirit can harden a person to the extent that he or she will delight in hurting the other.

With the powerful downdraft caused by the buildup of fiendish imps (▼) collecting in the "relatives" area of their relationship, it is now easy to forecast what is going to happen as their cutting comments become more deliberate. We have now a "wind shear" in the shared atmosphere.

Dan and Alice had been married for eight years. They were both looking forward to a special evening together. Alice left work early to fix supper, and Dan was to be home by 6:00. Around 4:00, Dan's mother called him at work with a crisis. She needed him to come by and fix something right away. He tried to protest, knowing that Alice would get angry, but his mother was quite upset, so he gave in and agreed to drop by. He decided to leave work early so that Alice would never find out. Alice needed something from the store, so she called Dan at 5:00, only to find out that he had already left. *He's gone to his mother's,* she thought angrily. *She knew we planned a special dinner tonight and is trying to mess it up!* By the time Dan came in at 6:00, the atmosphere had turned into bitterness. "How could you stop at that old bag's house on our anniversary?" Alice began. It actually felt good for Alice finally to call his mother an "old bag," since she could see how that offended Dan. Dan recoiled and shot back, "At least my mother can be warm and kind! You're nothing but a hard, cold nag!" The way he said "hard, cold nag" made Dan feel better. He didn't care how it made Alice feel. After a few more exchanges of bitterness, the rest of the meal was eaten in silence.

Weather Patterns after 10 Years

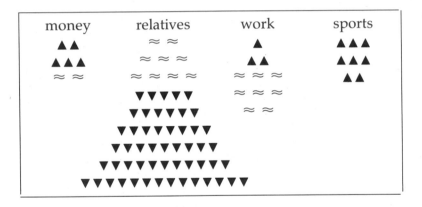

An inverted weather pattern has taken control of the home. Stagnation dominates. The next stage in their relationship is all too easy to forecast. As the inversion becomes entrenched and expands, bad moods become harder and harder to shift. Take another look at Dan and Alice five years later as theirs became truly a "household divided against itself" (Matt. 12:25):

> They stopped talking and began to communicate by writing notes. They had stopped touching several months earlier. It was obvious that they no longer wanted to be together. Grad-

ually the hostility shifted to its coldest form—total disinterest in the other person with only occasional sarcasm. Each still affected the other's mood, but they could no longer shift the bad mood between them. They lost hope that they could again be happy together. With that realization, they divorced.

The bad spirit (▼) that dominated in the shared space between Dan and Alice is now a separate entity, remaining after the relationship is no longer active. The power of the bad spirit can even increase with time. Five years after their divorce, the ugly, cold force with its atmospheric inversion hung there between them as strong as ever.

It had been five years since the divorce, but when Alice saw Dan walk into the back of the church at their daughter's wedding rehearsal, a wave of nausea hit her. She quickly turned away before he saw her, but all the old feelings were stirred up instantly. The sight of him thoroughly disgusted her. She did not look at him throughout the rehearsal and stayed as far away as possible, but she was constantly aware of his presence. It felt like an ugly, cold force coming from his direction. It destroyed her ability to enjoy this special event.

A Bad Spirit in Operation

A bad spirit born out of the downward flow of trapped energy has its own way of operating. *Once formed, the spirit then has an independent power of its own.* And one of this spirit's most fearful threats is its ability to *disguise itself.* Twisted and disguised by the devil's hands, it can now live as a diffuse, negative attitude free to influence other areas of a person's life (2 Cor. 11:14).

Perhaps the most powerful and destructive spiritual

force lies in the energy of these unresolved bad spirits. They now reside within the individual, separated from the original relationship, free to wreak havoc in disguised forms. Such destructive spirits can move within families or even within whole cultures. They become the breeding ground for negative energy, passed on from parent to child. Such bad spirits, separated from their source, are the basis for deep, lasting family evil. Take a look at Robert and Elaine's next-door neighbor, Larry:

> A strange feeling came over Larry. He deeply regretted it later, but at the moment when his young son stood there in defiance, he lost control. A form of deep anger came over him without warning, and at that moment Larry wanted to inflict pain on his son. He picked him up and slammed him against the wall so hard that his son was stunned for a few minutes. The intensity of his anger was truly frightening.

The destructive anger that Larry felt toward his defiant son was totally inappropriate to the situation. It came from another source. Deep within Larry's spirit was the unresolved rage he felt for the senseless beatings he had received during many of his own father's drunken episodes. He now carried this anger over in his own spirit as a force (fiendish or demonic IMPs) that could shift his mood dramatically downward at any time.

Defusing Potential Storms

Everyone accumulates unstable areas or places of emotional sensitivity caused by unresolved hurt. A greater awareness of the potential trouble spots—these hidden storm cells—increases the chance of keeping them from gaining the destructive power necessary to affect the weather within the shared atmosphere.

It is important to check your past for times when you

were repeatedly put down. Recall specific situations for which you can still vividly feel embarrassment, frustration, or hurt. Any bitter feelings or loss of respect toward the source of these retained feelings is a clear and direct indication of potential problems. It is so much easier to rega rd others as attacking you than to reveal the disguised storm cells that have built up in yourself. It is easier to see the "speck" in the other p erson's eye and pay no attention to the "plank" in your own eye (Matt. 7:3).

Chapter 5: Weather Watch Activities

1. Check your reaction to hurt feelings in present relationships. See if you can become more aware of the history of your emotional reactions.

   a. Let a situation come to mind that happened in the last few days. What feeling stayed with you?
   b. Now think of a time when you were left with this same feeling, perhaps in another relationship.
   c. Think back again to when you were growing up. Did you ever have this same feeling back then? Think over that situation and become aware of the history of that feeling.
   d. Go through this same process with other emotions that you typically end up with. Begin to realize that all of your current emotions have a history to them.

2. Unresolved conflicts can come back to your mind at strange times and disturb your peace of mind. Keep track of what is powerful enough to shift your mood when it comes back to your mind. Note especially those things that can disturb your sleep. These are the "demons" that you bring to your present relationships.

3. Think back and see if you can recall important disagreements or bad feelings your parents had toward each other. In subtle ways these cracks in their shared spirit

show up within your own spirit. These same themes or bad feelings have a way of showing up in your reactions to your own family.

4. Think back over the past year. See if you can come up with the times you have have thought privately, *Boy, she is treating me just like my mother used to,* or *He is so lazy, just like my father was.* Think of all the ways your spouse is like one of your parents. Then realize that you carry your reactions to these situations over from your background.

5. As a way of looking at the differences that could produce twists in your relationship with another person, talk over the following background situations. Note especially where the largest differences occur and then look for problems the two of you have encountered in these areas.

I. Set ways of doing things—what happened when . . .
   A. you did something wrong?
   B. you asked for money?
   C. you talked back to Dad or Mom?
   D. you achieved something?

II. Strategies developed—what worked for you? How did you learn to respond when . . .
   A. you wanted something?
   B. you tried to avoid work?
   C. you got someone upset?
   D. you got angry?

III. Subtle family messages—what did you grow up believing . . .
   A. about God?
   B. about premarital sex?
   C. about who your ideal person might be?

IV. Your model for family life—what usually happened when . . .
   A. you were on vacation?
   B. there was a crisis?
   C. your parents argued?

6. Check your significant past relationships for hurt feelings—for times when you were repeatedly put down and for specific situations that come back to your mind in which you can still vividly feel the embarrassment, frustration, or hurt. Any bitter feelings or loss of respect toward that person are clear and direct indicators of unresolved hurt. Consider each of your relationships and realize that these bitter feelings that you are carrying around are unresolved. Have the other family member do the same thing, if you wish.

7. Make a chart of feelings that you have carried over from your past, like the chart on Dan's background in the chapter. Have the other family member also complete such a chart, if you wish.

8. Compare your two charts and do some weather forecasting. Decide on the basis of the charts which areas will have good weather and which areas will become turbulent and troublesome between the two of you.

9. Separately do a complete map of the areas of your relationship with the other family member. Put in all of the carry-overs, and make the map look something like the one in the chapter on the shared space between Dan and Alice. Compare maps and come to agreement as to which sensitive areas in your family relationship you will learn how to confront in the next chapter.

10. Make similar charts for the relationships between other members of your family. Become aware of all of the sensitive areas in these relationships so you will know what needs to be confronted in the next chapter.

Notes

1. The concept of a "demon" in classical Greek literature suggests that such damage to the spirit of an individual through past unresolved hurt leaves its demonic carry-over in the emotional substructure of the individual. It will show up in other relationships when these deep

emotions get aroused. (See Rollo May, *Love and Will* [New York: Norton, 1969].)

2. A good way of conceptualizing strong carry-over feelings (like those of Dan and Alice) is to see them as emotions that have gotten stuck at an earlier age. These feelings are therefore often immature and cause mood shifts within the individual that resemble those of a child. It is as though "a little kid" (mischievous IMP) kicks up inside the person and takes control of the mood. Open expression of these carry-over feelings allows them to mature.

3. Even though many background problems can be cleared up by looking at them together with others in your family, there is a time when therapy is helpful to get to the subtle or deeply serious conflicts. Sexual and physical abuse or an alcoholic parent usually produces deeply serious inner spiritual problems.

4. A look at the history of families can be both encouraging and frightening. A grandparent's good spirit, for example, can show up in the loving personalities of offspring through many generations. On the other hand, alcoholism, affairs, abuse, or even a bitter marital relationship can also show up in the troubled lives of offspring to come.

Before You Read Chapter 6

Have you . . .

. . . ever been trapped in a bad mood?
Look at Romans 6:1–14.
What do you need to help shift those moods? Whatever you do, do not let a bad mood stay around for days. Venture into the bad weather—with God's help!

. . . ever wondered what it takes to shift a mood?
Look at Luke 18:9–14.
Who confessed? Whose mood was uplifted? Bad feelings don't give up easily. Watch out! God's Spirit just might soften up the hard places in your spirit!

. . . ever dragged a bad spirit into the light of day?
Look once more at Ephesians 4:15–16.
Speak the "truth in love." Confront the sensitive issue in the right spirit. Do it. Grow in spirit!

. . . ever felt a need for a "breath of fresh air" around your home?
Look at Ephesians 2:1–10.
Who causes the dead air to stagnate in your house? God's spirit "makes us alive together." That's fresh air! That's forgiveness! Go ahead! Hug each other again!

Chapter 6

Beyond Turbulence:
Breaking the Stagnation
of a Bad Spirit

The atmospheric inversion struck again at the Spring household. The mood had been good most of the week since Robert and Elaine went on their escape weekend. But the subject of money came up again. One of Elaine's friends happened to mention that she had run into Robert at the mall. Elaine could not remember Robert going there, so that evening she asked, "What were you doing at the mall? Sally mentioned that she saw you there." Robert felt that sinking feeling again in his chest as he answered, "Oh, nothing really." Sensing his defensiveness, Elaine immediately got suspicious. "How much money did you spend?" Robert gave no reply. Getting all upset inside, Elaine started digging, "I know you had $50 in your billfold yesterday. How much do you have left?" With that Robert exploded, "Why do I always have to answer to you? Get off my case!" Elaine knew that he had hidden his spending from her again and felt an old, deep bitterness take over her chest. A wave of disgust came over her as she looked at him.

Over a period of time the space where the shared spirit lives naturally gets cluttered with negative IMPs.

Gradually this clutter has an increasingly stagnating effect on the weather patterns of the home. That is the norm. A relationship can start out close and warm, but over a period of several years the sediment of unresolved conflicts covers the warmth and love.

Clearing up misunderstanding as it occurs is essential for any relationship; it will work against the natural tendency for bad weather to dominate. Reconciling the differences between family members keeps the spirit healthy and brings a creative edge to the family unit.

Though it is healthy for the home atmosphere to keep the air cleared, sin will inevitably enter in, as it did in the Spring family. The devil is crafty in getting us to hold onto our grudges and nurse our hurt feelings and pride. The gradual layering of emotional sediment is both subtle and diabolic.

Clearing the Bad Air

When a bad spirit has entered a family relationship, the family has a serious spiritual problem. The bad spirit cannot be allowed to remain. You have seen in the previous chapter the deadly consequences of letting a bad spirit take over an area of a relationship and cause a deadly downdraft in the home atmosphere.

A bad spirit cannot be changed directly into a good spirit. It is impossible for your attitude toward another person to go directly from disgust and bitterness to love and appreciation. The bad spirit must first be broken. Then the broken spirit can be changed into a good spirit.

When hard feelings form within family relationships through sin and threaten to alter the attitudes of the family members toward each other, the counsel and power of the Holy Spirit are needed to fight against this force of evil. The Spirit calls to confession and breathes the fresh air of forgiveness into the hardened places of the relationship. The process:

1. Soften up the hard places in one's own spirit as

the Holy Spirit calls the person to confess the sin and to receive and rely on the forgiveness that Jesus won for us all (1 John 1:8–2:2).

2. Gather in the name of Christ to confront the bad spirit (▼) with this attitude of *confession*. Confrontation deliberately raises the sensitive issue, causing the reappearance of the anxiety and hurt of the turbulent spirit (≈), but it now happens in the right spirit.

3. Stay with the sensitive topic, listening and struggling together to clear up the turbulence of the hurt feelings. With the Holy Spirit in control of the atmosphere, a new understanding can emerge, making the updraft (▲) of *forgiveness* possible.

The outcome sounds good, but the process is hard and can be frightening. The strategy outlined above suggests that sensitive areas be deliberately opened up—that turbulent weather actually be invited in. No wonder most people try to stay away from those areas that immediately shift the mood! Who wants to risk changing the atmosphere when things are finally going fairly well? Pilots go out of their way to avoid the powerful downdraft of a wind shear.

Deliberately Producing Bad Weather in the Home

You know the power of an atmospheric inversion (▼) around your home. For Robert and Elaine, money produced a powerful downdraft. Normally, you try to avoid those adverse topics, but somehow they tend to get activated anyway and end up controlling the weather around your home.

In order to break the power of these inversions over the family atmosphere, they must be deliberately activated in a controlled atmosphere. In this way the energy of the bad spirit (▼) can be converted into a good spirit (▲). The same area that could breed the most vicious storms can become the center of a good weather system, bringing warmth and closeness.

Let's go back to the weather chart of Robert and Elaine. Since they have learned how to communicate better, the weather patterns have improved remarkably around their home. Although they have resolved some of their conflicts, several issues can still produce strong turbulence ($\approx$). And one area under a critical inversion ($\blacktriangledown$) continues to produce a dramatic downdraft in the weather around their home.

Current Weather Chart between Robert and Elaine

family time	discipline	money
▲ ▲ ▲	▲ ▲ ▲	▲ ▲
▲ ▲ ▲ ▲	▲ ▲	
▲ ▲ ▲ ▲ ▲	▲	
▲ ▲ ▲ ▲		≈ ≈ ≈
		▼ ▼ ▼
≈ ≈ ≈	≈	▼ ▼ ▼ ▼
		▼ ▼ ▼ ▼
▼ ▼ ▼ ▼ ▼ ▼		

Robert and Elaine must deliberately activate the inversion being formed in the turbulent atmosphere of money, knowing that the mood will shift easily when this sensitive topic comes up. Before activating this force, Robert and Elaine must be prepared and united lest the downdraft ($\blacktriangledown$) overwhelm their attempt.

Internal Preparation to Activate Bad Weather

There is no way for the family to work together in a sensitive area if their spirits are not ready to be united. A bitter or resentful spirit will only make more trouble when a sensitive subject is brought up. So something must first be done with the individual spirits before going any further.

Since pride is at stake, breaking a bad internal spirit is nearly impossible. A bad spirit was formed by hurt feelings that finally hardened into disgust for another person. The bad spirit then disguises itself, putting the blame on the other person for one's own bad feelings. Since the bad feelings are so easily justified, it is virtually impossible to perceive them as wrong.

Elaine had no trouble justifying her lack of trust in Robert. After all, he spent their money again and again behind her back. Her lack of respect for him in this area was fully justified. She saw nothing wrong with her feelings; Robert just had to change. Robert also had no trouble justifying his resentment towards Elaine. After all, she had treated him again and again as if his feelings did not count. It was humiliating for him to check with Elaine before buying anything. He saw nothing wrong with his feelings; Elaine just had to change.

Call to Confession

So the bad spirit within must be changed to a broken spirit. This is a *big* change that would never occur by itself. Think of someone who arouses disgust within you. Can you imagine ever having good, warm, positive feelings toward that person? You cannot do this by an act of your will. The Holy Spirit must make this incredible change. Working through God's Word, the Holy Spirit breaks the bad spirit by turning you to see that *hard feelings, no matter how justified, are sinful* and grieve God's spirit (Eph. 4:30–32). The Holy Spirit calls to confession.

Confession totally changes attitudes; it raises us above our own hurt feelings and opens our eyes to the importance of the family relationships. Confession involves two things: (1) a change in attitude so that we admit that our sin is sin and express our willingness to work together to clear the air; (2) a faithful confidence that the Lord's word of forgiveness to us, because it is guaranteed and sealed by the death of His Son, is as firm and sure as if we had heard it from the lips of God Himself.

Confession must start within one's own spirit. Until the hard stagnant areas inside the spirit have been softened through confession, one cannot approach the shared space with the right spirit. Without this softening of spirit, there is no desire for reconciliation—only a desire to protect one's own pride and to inflict more hurt.

A good way to confess is on your knees in prayer, asking God to break the hardness of your spirit. "The sacrifices of God are a broken spirit; a broken and contrite heart, O God, you will not despise" (Ps. 51:17). When you can say, "God, have mercy on me, a sinner" (Luke 18:13), there is a proper attitude of confession. The Holy Spirit has helped soften up a hard place within your spirit. Then you can pray, "Renew a steadfast spirit within me" (Ps. 51:10).

The Powerful Updraft of Forgiveness Changes Your Mood

> I pray that out of his glorious riches he may strengthen you with power through his Spirit in your inner being, so that Christ may dwell in your hearts through faith. (Eph. 3:16–17)

This renewal is a miracle. And it actually changes your attitude and outlook. A show of respect from another person will always lift up your spirit. You receive a feeling of worth and acceptance. This is what shifts your mood upward (▲).

God shows deep respect for you by strengthening you "with power through His Spirit in your inner being" (Eph. 3:16) and letting you know your importance to Him. This will shift your mood upward (▲). "And by him we cry, 'Abba, Father.' The Spirit himself testifies with our spirit that we are God's children" (Rom. 8:15–16). By analogy, this is the same thing that happens to a child's mood when a parent grabs the child, gives a big hug, and says with deep feeling, "I love you!"

But how can God do this? Normally when someone has been hurt or sinned against in a relationship, the hurt has to be reconciled before love can flow again. In the case of our relationship with God, our sin has hurt and angered Him. His first reaction to us should be anger, pointing out our shortcomings and deflating our spirits. We certainly deserve such a reaction from God because of our sin. And if all we saw was His anger, we would rather run away than be pulled toward Him.

But God so loved his family that he sent His Son, Jesus Christ, to change all of this. Christ's death for our sins means that God does not count our sins against us (2 Cor. 5:19). As God touches our spirits through His Holy Spirit, we are uplifted by His love and warmth. *The Holy Spirit, not our own hard feelings (sinful nature), has control over our mood:* "You, however, are controlled not by the sinful nature but by the Spirit, if the Spirit of God lives in you" (Rom. 8:9). This is God's gift to us through baptism, when He made us a part of His family.

When God communicates the good, warm feelings of His love, He lifts us up above our own hurt feelings. This updraft mysteriously "evens up" our side of the relationship so that we no longer have to "get even!" This action on His part allows us to rise above the destructive situation. We are enabled to reach out with a good spirit, showing warmth and love to others. When the spirits of individual family members are warmed, the family is capable of being united in spirit. Then the sensitive, hurtful area of the relationship can be confronted.

Shared Preparation to Activate Bad Weather

When you are ready to tackle one of the sensitive topics in your relationship, set a time and place for your discussion. Begin with prayer, gathering in Christ's name, remembering that you are part of God's family through baptism. Let the mood have a sacred quality to it, praying together that the Holy Spirit would take control of the atmosphere as you struggle together.

The process that the Holy Spirit uses to change turbulence ($\approx$) into warmth and love ($\blacktriangle$) is *truth spoken in love*. "Speaking the truth in love" (Eph. 4:15) means that you will risk expressing what has been hurtful for the sake of the spirit. When you do this, you are in "confession," acknowledging that there are problems in the relationship. Doing this "in love" means that you are not pointing your finger at the other person but raising the issue to clear things up.

Speaking the truth in love has the ability to clear the air and restore the updraft ($\blacktriangle$) of a good spirit to the shared space. When this happens, God has once again performed a miracle in that shared space. He has restored a new and right spirit to dominate the weather of the family atmosphere!

> As for you, you were dead in your transgressions and sins, in which you used to live when you followed the ways of this world and of the *ruler of the kingdom of the air, the spirit* who is now at work in those who are disobedient. . . . Because of his great love for us, God, who is rich in mercy, *made us alive* with Christ even when we were dead in transgressions. (Eph. 2:1–5)

The "ruler of the kingdom of the air" is the diabolic force at work in the shared space. And do not underestimate the power of this evil force. If you think that by your own reason or strength you can change what happens in that shared space, you are badly mistaken. You cannot create a new and right spirit within this space; only God's Spirit has the power to do that. What you can do is trust that God's Spirit will work through each of your spirits to

101

clear up the shared space so that you can be alive together again. And you can sit down with the other person with an attitude of confession, "speaking the truth in love."

When a bad spirit has been confessed and forgiven, a different form of positive energy is generated. This positive energy (▲) of a reconciled spirit is unique in its power to maintain a good atmosphere in the relationship. After a couple has struggled and finally, with God's help, has achieved reconciliation, the connecting effect can be intense. When confession and forgiveness have occurred, a cross of reconciliation is left in the shared space. What a powerful updraft this creates in the home!

A cross in the shared space signifies Christ's love and redemption through Him. Where there is a cross in the shared space, deep understanding has occurred. This deep understanding greatly diminishes the potential for future misunderstanding and hard feelings in this area. This does not mean that conflict will no longer occur, but the relationship now has a tremendous advantage. The memory of the reconciliation will make it much easier to look at the shared space for the problem rather than at the other person.

To put it another way, the force of evil has been conquered by the cross of Jesus Christ. Therefore, as Christians, we live in the hope that God can take even the most painful areas in our family history and turn them into areas where the deepest closeness can occur. "And we know that in all things God works for the good of those who love him" (Rom. 8:28).

Specific Skills for Activating Bad Weather

Specific skills that help activate sensitive areas of a relationship are "personalizing" and "concretizing." Instead of going right into the middle of this highly turbulent area, approach it by focusing on one *concrete* event. Stick to that one event and let each person react to it *personally*.

Avoid approaching an area with an opening sentence

like "Yes, let's talk about your overreaction to everything!" The atmosphere will change immediately and produce a defensive and blaming situation. A better opening would be "Let's talk about last night. What were you feeling when we got the phone call?" With this concrete focus and personal expression of emotion, there is a much better chance of reconciliation.

Another important practical navigation aid is to look for the first time when there were hurt feelings in this area. Usually a vivid memory of an event lies at the bottom of a downdraft (▼). Perhaps something precious was lost, such as a dream, a hope, an ideal, or self-esteem.

You can only go back to this powerful original hurt when much of the other space is cleared out. Otherwise, it is too powerful. It is also helpful to experience working together as you clear out less sensitive areas. Then you can venture deeper into the area to find that vivid memory.

Robert and Elaine got that needed experience as they ventured into bad weather to tackle one of the big remaining fiendish IMPs involving their past sexual relationship:

> Robert and Elaine deliberately set aside time one evening to have a heart-to-heart talk about their sexual problems. When they sat down together, they held hands and began with prayer. Robert then admitted being discouraged because at times Elaine seemed disinterested in his advances. Elaine acknowledged her lack of desire but did not know what to do. Robert then asked if this had always been the case. Elaine replied, "I don't know why, but I have unsettled feelings about making love." After talking further, Robert remembered that Elaine had been quite responsive when they first dated. He then asked Elaine if there was something vivid about their sexual contact before they got married. She became visibly shaken and grew quiet. He gently asked

what she was remembering right then, and out it came. Elaine began, "I remember just like it was yesterday. We were in my room listening to music. My parents were gone, and we started fooling around. I did not feel right about it but was afraid to stop because I was afraid of losing you. You told me that this was very important to see if we were compatible. So I let you go all the way. Afterwards, I felt so cheap and dirty. I did not sleep all night and did not want to see you the next day." As she talked, tears came to her eyes and she said, "I lost something precious that night, and it was not what I had dreamed it would be." Elaine could barely see through her tears. Robert was listening closely, and he could feel his throat tighten. His voice cracked as he said, "I didn't realize how important that was. I was so insensitive that night, and what I did was wrong. Forgive me."

This was the moment of the original hurt, remembered in its personal and concrete form. With that memory, the problem in this area finally began to clear after 15 years. They could actually feel the wall going down when this vivid event was confessed and forgiven. Sexual intimacy was free to become a deeper area of warmth and good contact at last.

Activating the Worst Weather

As Robert and Elaine continued working on their turbulent ($\approx$) areas, they found a noticeably positive effect on the atmosphere around the home. The mood would not shift downward as often. When it did, the family could come back together and shift it back more easily. Their relationship was developing a fair-weather pattern.

With the atmosphere of their relationship now more stable, they were ready to tackle the most powerful mood-shifting area of their shared space. Robert and Elaine deliberately activated the sensitive area of money in the right spirit—with their relationship in good working order:

Elaine was paying the bills one night and asked Robert about a $30 item he had charged. He said that it was none of her business. Normally, this would have been the start of bad weather. But this time they agreed to talk it over. They went to the special place in their home that they had started using for talks like these. They held hands and prayed together. Then they deliberately focused only on the $30 item. Robert started, "I'm afraid to ask, but what all went through your mind when you first saw the bill tonight?" Elaine replied, "My heart sank. You had promised not to charge anything without my knowledge." Robert then asked Elaine to tell him about her anxiety over money. He listened to Elaine's fears and for the first time began to realize that Elaine did not bring up the subject just to make him feel guilty. Elaine then asked Robert what he was feeling when he said, "It is none of your business." Robert replied, "I felt that old, familiar pain in my stomach—like a sinking feeling. I knew I would not get a chance to explain. I had already been judged, so why even try?" The next five minutes Elaine listened as Robert opened up his feelings of being controlled. Elaine heard him and for the first time began to realize that Robert cut her off because the subject was so sensitive for him and left him feeling powerless.

The subject of money was not resolved that evening, but one of the bad feelings (▼) was confessed, understood, and changed to a reconciled, positive (†) memory. One piece of the downdraft was converted to an updraft, and others were to follow until their shared space had a much different weather pattern to it.

The Reconciled Space between Robert and Elaine

family time	discipline	money
▲▲▲▲	▲▲▲▲	▲
▲▲▲▲▲	▲▲▲	▲▲
▲▲▲▲▲▲	▲▲▲	
▲▲▲▲▲	▲▲	≈ ≈ ≈
	≈ ≈	≈ ≈
†		▼▼
		†

Their relationship now had new life to it. Bad moods no longer had the same control over the family spirit. The *strong force* of a good spirit was now more in control of the atmosphere of their home.

> Bear with each other and forgive whatever grievances you may have against one another. Forgive as the Lord forgave you. And over all these virtues put on love, which binds them all together in perfect unity. (Col. 3:13–14)

Chapter 6: Weather Watch Activities

1. Talk a bit about the truly bad spirits you have encountered in your life. Think of how they distorted all communication. Have you ever thought of the devil in connection with this bad spirit? Did you feel the force of evil in that situation?

2. Did the power of the bad spirits increase over time, that is, did it become harder to reconcile the relationship? Was there a time when it could have been more easily reconciled? Isn't it true that over time those feelings just get colder and produce more rigid perceptions, making reconciliation more and more difficult?

3. Now work on relationships within your family. First adopt a firm rule for family life: "Never go to bed angry." This is one of the most important Scriptural guidelines for the health of family ties. Apply that rule by asking each night as you gather together, "Does anyone have anything that they need to say before we go to bed?" Start tonight!

4. Now look at the map you drew of the shared space from the previous chapter. Let the existence of the map be a constant reminder that family problems are mutual problems. Remind each other that when you point one finger of blame at another, three are pointed back at you. Instead, point at the map of your shared spirit. In that way acknowledge that the hurt feelings involved are a shared problem in your relationship.

5. Take the map and get ready to tackle one of the mildly sensitive areas. Make sure you keep the weather under control! Don't let the mood shift on you, if you can help it. Let God's Spirit control the weather for you.

   a. Agree on an issue that you are going to talk over. Then separately pray that the Holy Spirit would soften up your spirit so that you can approach this sensitive area in the right spirit. When both of you are ready, go on to the next step.

   b. Focus on the most recent event related to the sensitive area and stick with that event *only* in your conversation. In this way help keep the weather under control. Otherwise the conversation can open up too many sensitive things at once.

   c. Sit across a table so you can look directly at each other. Get out 10 coins so that each of you can have 5 to start with. The person who starts the conversation pushes one coin to the middle of the table (figuratively to the point of the shared space) and keeps the finger on the coin.

   d. That person starts with the words "I know that you might see it differently." This gives the listener the permission to have different feelings and will help the listening process. That person then expresses his/her feeling about the event under consideration with the words "Let me tell you how I reacted inside to that situation." (Look at the examples of the chapter for ways to express the feelings without automatically blaming the other person.)

e. The listener then has to repeat what was said and acknowledge the right of the other person to feel that way. If the first person feels understood, and the feelings are being taken seriously, the coin stays on the table, signifying that the two of you are building an understanding in that shared space. If, however, the listener discounts or "buts" what was said, the coin goes to the side, signifying that the issue is still being avoided.

f. Then the listener pushes one of his/her coins out to the center of the table, keeps the finger on the coin as before, and begins with the words "I understand what you feel about the situation, *and* let me add what was going through my mind when this happened." The use of the word *and* rather than *but* is critical for the building process. Each comment must build on the other and not tear it down.

g. After all 10 coins have been used, the two of you can visually see whether an understanding about the situation is being built in the shared space, or whether the issue is being deflected. If the coins are between you, that sensitive area should feel warmer and more free, indicating that reconciliation is starting to occur.

6. Repeat this process for other concrete situations in the same area of the map. The goal is that the process will get down to the point of the original hurt so that it can then be forgiven. (Be patient! It may take many discus-

sions.) When that happens, take your map and put an updraft symbol (▲) to replace one of the turbulent (≈) ones or a cross (†) to replace one of the downdraft (▼) symbols. You can graphically demonstrate that a new, powerful force of good now lives in the shared space where a turbulent or a bad spirit once held control. Now thank God for the power of reconciliation through his Son, Jesus Christ.

Notes

1. The techniques of personalizing and concretizing in order to resolve unfinished business are Gestalt techniques of therapy (W. Passons, *Gestalt Approaches in Counseling* [New York: Holt, Rinehart, and Winston, 1975]). The concept of "energy flow" in Gestalt psychology has some similarities to the concept of "spirit" presented in this book.

2. Scriptural insight suggests that the Holy Spirit does not work "immediately" in the shared space but works in the spirits of each of the persons. The Spirit, as the Spirit of Christ, brings the reconciliation of God that Jesus won by bringing us the good news of forgiveness, life, and salvation. This blood-bought reconciliation with God enables us and directs us to "be reconciled" to each other. God's Holy Spirit is the Spirit of reconciliation, who enables us to confront the problem in a loving and constructive manner in each other's presence. The shift of atmosphere brought about by Christian confession and forgiveness is thus one of the gifts of the Holy Spirit to bring love, joy, and peace back into the relationship (the fruit of the Spirit).

3. Much of this chapter can be applied to the spiritual counselor. Such a counselor is to aid the spirits, both individual and collective, of the family. It is critical that the counselor stay aligned in the center of the relationship when working with a couple or a family and not get ma-

nipulated into seeing one side or the other better. In that way the concern for the spirit or for the family ties is maintained. Another directive to the counselor is not to listen to bad spirits (hard, bitter feelings) but to confront and break them. A bad spirit cannot be reconciled until it has been broken and becomes a broken spirit. A final directive is not to be harsh with a broken spirit but rather be quick to forgive when confession has occurred!

Before You Read Chapter 7

Have you . . .

. . . ever noticed how powerful being "one in spirit" is?
Look at Philippians 2:1–5.
The "fellowship" of the Spirit is real—and mysterious.
Things work right when the family spirit is strong. It
is the strong force.

. . . ever felt that your house was divided against itself?
Look at Matthew 12:25–32.
Do you ever yell and scream? Did it really help? Or
did it just get everyone in a bad mood? That is the
weak force.

. . . ever faced rebellious children? I suspect so.
Look at Philippians 1:27–30.
Kids desperately need rules but will test them out.
And they will find the cracks; you can bet on that! Do
you stand together, "firm in one spirit"? That's what
the kids need.

. . . ever wished that people would take notice when you
speak? Or do your own kids ignore you?
Look at Ephesians 3:16–19.
God strengthens your spirit—that's the strong force.
That's personal authority. Then yes means yes and no
means no.

Chapter 7

Living in the Right Spirit: The Strong Force Creates Fair Weather for the Family

Robert and Elaine would never forget that night. It was their 20th wedding anniversary and a special celebration of their renewed spirit. It started with candlelight dinner. Robert kept writing "Elaine" on his napkin. It was as if he had rediscovered her. When they looked at each other, time stood still as a powerful force pulled them both into the depth of the moment. Then there were the hours spent by the fireplace gazing into the flames, snuggled against each other. Neither wanted the warmth and closeness of the evening to end. The deep bonding feelings would be remembered for the rest of their lives.

The Mysterious Power of a Good Spirit

When the two people are together and a good spirit flows between them, something additional is present in that space that can lift both of them to heights they could not reach alone. They are tapping into spiritual energy, the lifting power (▲) of a good spirit.

He made known to us the *mystery* of his will according to his good pleasure, which he purposed in Christ, to be put into effect when the times will have reached their fulfillment—to bring all things in heaven and on earth *together* under one head, even Christ. (Eph. 1:9–10)

The word *mystery* does not mean something that cannot be solved but that which is deep, powerful, and meaningful in life. God's purpose and will come alive as the Holy Spirit brings the family together.

If you have any encouragement from being united with Christ, if any comfort from his love, if any fellowship with the Spirit, if any tenderness and compassion, then make my joy complete by being like-minded, having the same love, *being one in spirit and purpose.* (Phil. 2:1–2)

"Being one in spirit" is the *strong force.* You will never see this force, but its presence is unmistakable. The strong force changes a house into a home. It makes the home a place of warmth and love where family members focus on "us" and "we" more than on "me" or "I." This is the basis for a strong fair-weather (▲) system.

The *weak force* is just the opposite: "Every . . . household divided against itself will not stand" (Matt. 12:25). The weak force encourages each person to look out after his/her own best interests, breeding jealousy, selfish ambition, dissension, envy, and disobedience (Gal. 5:20; Eph. 2:2). This force produces the weak (≈) or rapidly deteriorating (▼) weather systems.

The Gathering Power of the Strong Force

A good spirit within the family is a powerful motivating force. It draws family members together, makes them want to be together, and refreshes the individual's spirit in the process: "We were especially delighted to see how happy Titus was, because his spirit has been refreshed by all of you" (2 Cor. 7:13). This mutual uplifting (▲) and encouragement by the strong force is one of the spiritual gifts that St. Paul writes about: "I long to see you so that I may impart to you some spiritual gift to make you strong—that is, that you and I may be mutually encouraged by each other's faith" (Rom. 1:11).

With the strong force of a good spirit present, the family stays together, not out of guilt or obligation but because it is uplifting (▲) to come back to laughter and warmth. No one can stay away from such an atmosphere for long.

In a fascinating way, the strong spirit commands *attention* and *respect*. When this force is present between two people, they are *attentive* to each other. Each one is totally *present* in the relationship. Used in this sense, *presence* refers to the degree to which the whole person is engaged in the interaction. This can vary from minimal presence required to carry on a surface conversation to almost 100 percent presence when in contact with a special person.

> It was obvious that Rose was bored with Diane's conversation. She would nod her head and then look away, as if to find something more interesting. She was just not listening. Just then Tim walked by. Her eyes suddenly brightened as she caught his eye. She interrupted Diane in midsentence to say to Tim, "How did it go?" At that moment, she shifted from 10 per cent to 100 per cent presence.

This concept of presence can be turned around. To assess the state of the spirit in any shared space, one can carefully observe the degree to which a person wants to be present to the other person. A strong desire to be present to the other person indicates that the strong force is there.

The strong spirit also commands *respect*. Two people look at each other totally differently in the presence of the strong force as compared to the weak force. The strong force (▲) will prompt two people to look up to each other;

the weak force (▼) will get them to look down at each other.

When two or more people are united in spirit, what they agree on is respected by others. If the agreement comes about when they are gathered in Christ's name, God will respect it: "I tell you that if two of you on earth agree about anything you ask for, it will be done for you by my Father in heaven. For where two or three come together in my name, there am I with them" (Matt. 18:19–20).

The Strong Force at Work in the Home

The strong spirit (▲) between husband and wife is the most powerful force within the family unit. It sets the climate for all the other relationships within the family. It is a firm strength that provides security and authority for the family.

The strong force between husband and wife lifts up the parents in the sight of the child, commanding the child's respect. When the two "stand firm in one spirit" (Phil. 1:27), there is "a demonstration of the Spirit's power" (1 Cor. 2:4) that becomes the true authority of the household. This force sets the rules for family life and establishes what *will* happen, not just what ought to take place.

A type of radar built into the child's spirit will detect and welcome the strong force for the authority and security that this force gives. This radar will also test any other force to see if it has the strong force behind it. If the radar detects that parental directives come from the weak force (≈), the child will push against them.

The strangest thing happens when the strong force is firmly in place. The child can *be* the child and like that position. The child must first find the strong force in order to function securely as a child. Without the strong force, the child will push against the authority of the parents, trying to find the secure place where the parents are united in spirit. Then the child can stop pushing and start being the child.

The good atmosphere that forms the strong force projects the same atmosphere into the child's own spirit. The strong force becomes a part of the child and provides the basis for the child's own self-discipline. These are the rules, boundaries, and values the child desperately needs to feel free and good within. The child's spirit always reflects some dimension of the spirit between the parents. To put it another way, by far the most important gift you can give to your children is that you "love one another" (1 John 4:7).

The strong force transmits the values of the parents to the children as it provides the inner strength for the child's spirit. The child will believe in what the strong force communicates.

The Weak Force between Two Parents

The weak force (▼) produces the downdraft that lowers the authority of the parents in the eyes of the child and causes diminished respect. If the weak force (≈) is present, the parents are not united. Each parent must use a threatening force to get the child to respond. Paradoxically, the weak force often gets expressed in a loud, angry way to overcome the disagreement of the other parent. Although the threats sound strong, the child's radar will detect the weakness behind them and will inevitably push against this weak force. The weak force must then become more and more threatening or guilt-producing to enforce the child's obedience.

The weak force (▼) pulls down the child's spirit. In so many situations, the child either rebels or becomes dispirited. The child's spirit inhales this bad atmosphere. Children raised in a stormy, hostile atmosphere will carry that bad atmosphere within them. They have great difficulty finding peace, warmth, and happiness within themselves. They become attracted to artificial, substitute means of producing the warmth or good feeling inside—

alcohol, drugs, sex, or peer acceptance.

The Spring family was finally able to deal with this weak force in their home:

> Dawn started rebelling when bedtime came around. Elaine tried to be firm but felt helpless as Robert ignored the situation. Elaine finally got angry with Robert and wondered, "Do you even care?" That made Robert upset. He stomped over to Dawn, physically carried her to her bed, and slammed the door. As she began screaming, Elaine got more upset at Robert for being so harsh and ended up going into Dawn's bedroom to calm her down.

It is easy to see that the weak force is present in the father's anger and the division between the parents. Dawn found the crack in their united front and was rebelling against the weak force.

Developing a Strong Force between Parents

The strong spirit, based on Christ's love for us, flows out of the love the parents have for each other—a love that struggles with conflicts until there is agreement. This creates a united front to present to the children.

> Robert and Elaine sat down and used their much-improved ability to communicate to come up with a bedtime procedure that they both could *agree* on. They sat their 5-year-old daughter down and said, *"We* want to talk to you." They then *looked at each other,* nodded their heads in *agreement,* and smiled at each other, visually *joining forces* with each other. As they looked back at Dawn, Robert spoke, *"We* have talked over your bedtime." Then Elaine continued, "Yes, and *we* have decided that you *will* be in your bed at 8:30." And Robert concluded, "And you *will*

stay in your bed at that time and go to sleep."
With that they looked back at each other, nodded
in *agreement*, and smiled. Dawn's radar was
going crazy. She looked back and forth, expect-
ing to see the usual pattern of disagreement, but
could only feel the united spirit. She seemed not
to like it but had nothing to say. A few minutes
later, she was happily playing, and at 8:30 that
night she went to bed without the usual rebel-
lion. She had met the strong force and was
warmed inside by the security it brought to the
family.

Developing a Strong Force with a Single Parent

The unity of spirit in Christ that exists between parents makes possible the strong force in the family. This
same strong force can also exist within the spirit of an
individual, based on the strength and conviction coming
from faith in Christ (Eph. 3:16).

The weak force ($\approx$) within a person is based on mixed
feelings and unresolved conflicts within—guilt, regret, and
uncertainty. St. Paul reflects: "When I planned this, did I
do it lightly? Or do I make my plans in a worldly manner
so that in the same breath I say, 'Yes, yes' and 'No, no'?"
(2 Cor. 1:17).

The presence of the weak force ($\approx$) inside a person
usually signals unresolved feelings carried over from past
bad relationships. The process of developing the strong
force ($\blacktriangle$) within includes clearing up these IMPs.

The best way is to go back to the other person, following the directives of Matt. 18:15–17. Face to face, work
to clear up the shared space. If this happens, you no longer
carry over the troublesome feelings from this relationship.

Alice grew to realize that even though she
was divorced from Dan, a reminder of him could
still have a dramatic effect on her mood. The in-

118

cident at their daughter's marriage made that clear to her. She did call Dan, wanting to talk, but Dan was bitter. He wanted nothing to do with her.

If the other person is not willing to talk things over, the shared space cannot be cleared up. But you can still clear up your half of the space so that you do not carry over these bad feelings into other relationships.

The sediment of emotions that builds up consists of hurt feelings. This makes the relationship seem out of balance; therefore you feel that you must hold on to the bitterness and resentment. Otherwise you feel that the other person has won. The bondage to sin is in part expressed as the atmospheric inversion (▼) of past bad spirits that trap us in our own emotions. Some people spend a lifetime trying to get even.

The natural downdraft (▼) of getting even must be broken by means of confession. Confession acknowledges that the bad feelings you still harbor are sinful and gets you beyond the usual justification for those bitter feelings.

Then you need help from a friend. The Holy Spirit is your friend (John 14:26) and often works through others. The updraft (▲) of the Holy Spirit lifts your spirit above the need to get even. As you feel loved and warmed as part of His family, the hurt is taken away and you can forgive. The shared space of the old relationship may still not be cleared up, but your half of it is.

Alice began talking to a friend from church. She had previously delighted in cutting Dan down, but now she took a deep look at her own hurt. It had been painful to lose her dream of a close, warm family. As she talked of her hurt and her dream, she started to heal. A new and right spirit began to form inside. With the renewal of a right spirit, Alice also began to relate differently to her children who were still at home. They encountered the strong force (▲) of her good spirit.

A strong force (▲) within the parent means that his/her spirit is united. There is no inner confusion and personal frustration that would give the child a double message. Any time the parent uses guilt or angry threats to get the child to respond, the weak force is at work.

The strong spirit is "sincere" (1 Tim. 3:8); "Yes" means yes, and "No" means no (James 5:12). "Simply let your 'Yes' be 'Yes,' and your 'No,' 'No'; anything beyond this comes from the evil one" (Matt. 5:37).

The strong force of authority is conveyed by a firm voice, kind but powerful eye contact, and clearly communicated messages. "Then Saul, who was also called Paul, filled with the Holy Spirit, looked straight at Elymas" (Acts 13:9). "Paul looked straight at the Sanhedrin" (23:1). This is the "courage" that others can observe (4:13) and marvel at. This is the strong force that Peter met when "the Lord turned and looked straight at" him (Luke 22:61).

The look, the tone of voice—the clear presence of the good spirit of the parent—conveys authority. Such contact helps the child feel secure and loved rather than pushed aside or put down. That mysterious impact is what the child yearns for. When the child thus meets the strong force (▲) of parental authority, it brings fair weather both to the family unit and within each family member.

> It still was not easy to be a single parent, but the mood had definitely changed in Alice's household. There were plenty of conflicts, but the shouting and rebellion were gone. And there were many more moments of warmth and tenderness.

The strong force is always a loving force, coming from the conviction of the parent(s) and pointed toward the good of the family or the child. It will always speak the truth in love (Eph. 4:15) and has concern for the good of the relationships involved. It is the force that seeks to build up (▲) and preserve the spirit—both individual and family.

And the child, sensing the loving spirit behind the force, will be comforted by its presence.

> "And over all these virtues put on love, which binds them all together in perfect unity" (Col. 3:14)

Chapter 7: Weather Watch Activities

1. Exercise some of your family ties by remembering times of closeness and fun together. Help your remembering with pictures or movies. Write down individually one special time when you felt the closest to each other and then share what you have written.

2. Exercise the family ties as part of God's family by writing down the times that you have felt closest to God—times you will never forget. The Holy Spirit will help you remember. "The Counselor, the Holy Spirit, whom the Father will send in my name, will teach you all things and will *remind* you of everything I have said to you" (John 14:26).

3. Think of one relationship as you were growing up that gave you the most warmth and acceptance—in which the spirit was good and you thoroughly enjoyed being with that person. Then thank God for touching your spirit with this person's love.

4. What do family bonds feel like? Remember the feeling when a family member was in trouble. Put down in your journal what it felt like when one of these bonds was broken or hurt through death or through a bad situation. The feelings go incredibly deep, don't they?

5. Check how much you were "present" today in each of your relationships. Your spirit is completely present if you are really caught up in the spirit of things. If you are bored or your mind is wandering, you are probably only 20 percent present. Notice how a good spirit makes it easy for you to be "all there."

6. What are the things you really want to do and the people you really want to be with? Notice the correlation between a good spirit and your wanting to be in that atmosphere. Which "spaces" do you enjoy the most?

7. Practice the strong force with another person. If it is with your spouse, deliberately set up the situation described in this chapter. Set the child in front of the two of you, look at each other and smile, then tell him/her what "we" have decided in a calm but firm voice, completing each other's sentences.

8. Notice the weak force when it emerges within the family spirit. Be able to spot this force clearly. Make a guess as to where the cracks are in your relationship with your spouse.

9. Also notice the weak force in yourself—when you feel that you have to yell or give in to resolve a problem. Make a guess as to where the cracks are in your own spirit (your own guilt or uncertainty that can be touched off).

10. Practice expressing the strong force from within yourself. Realize that this strong force comes from your own integrity and deep convictions as to what is good for your child. Before reacting to your child, pause and make a good decision within as to what is best for him/her. Then practice expressing your decision in a firm but loving manner.

11. Apply the directive of the chapter to "clean up your half of the space" to one of your past bad relationships. Talk over that relationship with a pastor, counselor, or friend. Through your own soul-searching and confession, clear up your part of that relationship.

12. Focus on the idea that the child inherits the relationship between his parents within his own spirit or that you carry around inside you the atmosphere that surrounded you as you grew up. Describe the spirit of that atmosphere. If it was a good one, thank God. If it was not such a good one, determine to work on it and ask for God's help. Realize that He wants you to live in an atmosphere of love and peace and that you pass this love on to others.

Notes

1. The concept of "synergy" or the energy that the family spirit brings to the individuals in the family unit is similar to the concept, developed by Maslow, that identification with others tends to promote energy within the individual (A. Maslow, *Motivation and Personality* [New York: Harper and Row, 1970]).

2. The concept that an individual's feelings about self (spirit) is dramatically affected by feedback from significant others (individuals who are important to the person) is a well-known observation of the field of social psychology (G. H. Mead, *On Social Psychology* [Chicago: University of Chicago Press, 1965]). In this way, the climate inside an individual is directly affected by the feedback climate of the immediate environment.

3. The concept that the child's spirit reflects the relationship between the parents is, to my knowledge, a novel idea. I firmly believe that the atmosphere inside a person is influenced by the atmosphere of the home, and the most influential relationship in terms of setting the mood for the household is the spirit between the parents.

4. It is possible to have the strong force within your spirit even though you are in a bad relationship. You do not have the power to change an unwilling partner, but you can stay "clean" on your side of the relationship. As you do not react in kind to the bad feelings coming from the other person, you "heap burning coals" (Rom. 12:20) on the other person's head that can make him/her stop and think. This can have a positive effect on the relationship over the long term.

Before You Read Chapter 8

Have you . . .

. . . ever felt that our culture is not spiritually healthy? Is there a good spiritual framework in families?

Once again, look at Ephesians 4:14–16.

The "supporting ligaments" are the family ties. Over a million families break up every year. Does that sound healthy?

. . . done something to keep your family spirit strong?

Look at Ephesians 2:19–22.

Just as muscles are strengthened by exercise, family ties need exercise. You need time together—prime time for the family. Do you have a family altar? Would you think about starting one? Your family needs all the help it can get!

. . . noticed how busy you are? Everyone is on a different schedule.

Look at Matthew 18:19–20.

Why not go where they are—anywhere "two or three" of you can gather together? What about a portable family altar—in the car, out to eat, with other church members, and even in a hot-air balloon?

Chapter 8

Renewing Your Family's Spirit: God in Control of the Weather in Your Home

Robert Spring was in a good mood. Dinner was over, and while everyone was sitting around the table, he got up and brought in a rose from its hiding place. He felt like kidding. "How is Mom like a rose?" he asked the children. "Hey! That's my name!" Rose chipped in. "Well, she's pretty," Dawn ventured. "And fragrant," Sonny added. "Yep, she is all of that—and more," Robert continued. "Notice the thorns? Handle gently, or else!" Elaine made a big show of protest and the whole family ended up laughing. "I like this good weather in our house," Dawn observed. "We used to fight at the table all the time." Elaine agreed: "I remember all too well when everyone wanted to get away from the table as soon as possible." "How can we keep the good weather around?" Rose asked; "I like it, too."

Prime Time for the Family

What controls the atmosphere in your home? Are the moods unpredictable? Do bad moods settle in and stay around for days? How can you change that?

You cannot control the weather in your home directly. The shared spirit controls the mood. But you can work on renewing the family spirit, and that will make quite a difference in the atmosphere.

This means developing a Christian lifestyle. Living in God's family means that the Holy Spirit helps with the weather. There is no quick fix as the culture seems to want and expect. It is a long-term building process that gradually has a positive effect (▲) on the weather. That is what the Spring family found out as they struggled together to rebuild their relationships.

> "Well, I have learned that good moods do not just happen," Robert began. "We can affect the weather around our home by keeping our spirits united." "What does that mean?" Dawn asked. "That means that we keep in touch with God and with each other. That means that we talk through things with Him and with each other," Robert answered. "Do you know how hard that is with all our schedules?" Elaine broke in. "Why not schedule some family time?" Rose asked. "I make a motion that we start tonight and make it 'prime time'!" Sonny exclaimed. " 'Prime time'—I like that term," Robert said. "That makes our time together the top priority."

And so the Spring family decided to schedule prime time together in connection with family devotions each evening. Dawn wanted a special place for family time in the living room. Rose came up with the idea of calling it "the family altar." Sonny made a cross and candlesticks to keep in that special place.

Weather Control: The Family Altar

The family altar gives the family time together to strengthen their relationships with each other and with

God. It is a time to work on the family spirit. The Spring family began to develop special time together once they learned how important it was to keep working on the good spirit that was emerging in their life together. They gathered in the living room right after supper each evening for "family time." Sonny was in charge of lighting the candles that stood next to the cross to signal that it was time to begin.

A good spirit is motivating, attractive, and energizing. If family time is boring or done out of duty, obligation, or guilt, something is wrong. Family altar time can be a time that everyone eagerly anticipates and that is missed when something else gets in the way. In the Spring family, if an evening was missed, Dawn would be the first to say, "When are we going to make up our family time?"

To make it uplifting and exciting, this must be a time when emotions are shared and things of deeper significance are discussed. In the Spring family, after a devotion each person was asked, "Well, what has been on your mind today?" You would be surprised at the deep and sensitive subjects that were openly expressed at this time.

Never make family time merely a routine reading of prepared material. Certainly you may use devotional aids and Biblical readings, but encourage spontaneous responses and questions. Seek a balance between respect for God's presence and open expression. Robert usually read a devotion with its Scripture passage. But he would often stop and say, "Well, any good thoughts brewing?"

Try singing and developing special family songs. Have family members make up their own lines to easy-to-sing tunes. The Spring family loved singing, "Dawn, do you love Jesus?" She would answer, "Yes, I love Jesus, for He first loved me." Let the creativity of the family shine forth in these songs.

And what about touch and movement? Sitting still and apart from each other can be deadly on the level of energy. Be creative and develop a format that attracts peo-

energy. Be creative and develop a format that attracts people to each other. In the Spring family Dawn was always sitting on someone's lap. Sometimes the family would act out a Bible scene. Often the family altar time led naturally into a fun time of joking and clowning around with one another.

Do not forget about humor. The Spring family found themselves teasing each other in good fun more and more as their spirit became stronger. They simply enjoyed each other and delighted in playing practical jokes on each other. They began doing special things for each other to celebrate important events.

Family Health and the Weather

The health of any family is directly related to the strength of its spiritual framework—the places where the family unit is "joined and held together . . . as each part does its work" (Eph. 4:16). This framework is expressed in the weather patterns that form within the dynamic, shared space.

What kind of weather patterns do we find within families today? Do most families generally experience good weather? Is there normally a good spirit within most households? If we took a random selection of homes, would we find a warm, caring, loving, and trusting atmosphere?

A Good Weather Pattern in the Home

family time	working together	discipline	money
▲	▲	▲	▲
▲ ▲ ▲	▲ ▲	▲ ▲	▲ ▲
▲ ▲ ▲ ▲	▲ ▲ ▲	▲ ▲ ▲	▲ ▲ ▲
≈ ≈ ≈	≈ ≈ ≈	≈ ≈ ≈	≈ ≈ ≈ ≈
≈ ≈	≈ ≈ ≈	≈ ≈ ≈	≈ ≈ ≈ ≈
	≈ ≈	≈ ≈	≈ ≈
		▼	▼ ▼

Or would we find animosity, jealousy, indifference, and an attitude of distrust that only looks out for the good of the individual? Sad to say, the following weather pattern is all too true of most families today:

A Bad Weather Pattern in the Home

family time	working together	discipline	money
	▲		
	≈ ≈ ≈	≈ ≈ ≈	≈ ≈
≈ ≈ ≈	≈ ≈ ≈	≈ ≈	▼▼▼▼
≈ ≈ ≈ ≈	≈ ≈ ≈	▼▼▼	▼▼▼▼
▼▼	▼▼▼▼	▼▼▼	▼▼▼
▼	▼▼▼	▼▼▼	▼▼▼
	▼▼	▼▼▼	▼▼

Powerful spiritual forces are at work in the places where people are bonded together in the family unit. These forces have rules of their own, affecting the weather patterns by changing the spiritual framework of the family.

Our culture has gone through an unhealthy period for families. The pervasive attitude that places personal happiness and individual rights above concern for relationships has taken its toll on the quality of family life. The depth of happiness and fulfillment that only a good spirit can provide is an elusive dream for too many people. The norm for our culture is bad weather (▼)—drug abuse, sexual promiscuity, self-centeredness, and greed—rather than good weather (▲)—contentment, warmth, and love.

In one sense, such self-centered attitudes have always characterized human culture. But in another sense, there has been a spiritual deterioration within the last several decades. Mobility has shifted concern away from community and personal integrity toward the rights of the individual and distrust for a person's word. The heady power of technological advance has shifted our belief system away from intangible, transcendent values toward tangible, success-oriented goals. For most people, scientific understanding has replaced spiritual wisdom.

The picture is not pretty as one looks at the deep connecting places within our culture. The spiritual foundation of our culture is in trouble. There is a critical inability to form good, lasting relationships. Divorce seems the preferred solution for those who look for happiness without the pain and emotional struggle that are the basis of deep relationships. With the extended family in shambles and the neighborhood made up of isolated units, individuals are forced to look out for themselves, defending their rights at every step.

The yearning for depth and closeness, though misdirected from God's purpose, remains within each person. Deep within the soul—beneath the frenzied pace of life, the drugged consciousness, and the obsessive drive for success—the desire for connection remains.

God Controls the Weather

Pitted against the powerful spiritual forces within our culture that seek to destroy the family unit, the family needs help for its spirit. And who can give spiritual help better than God Himself? His Holy Spirit has the power to affect the atmosphere of your home.

> I will ask the Father, and he will give you another Counselor to be with you forever—the Spirit of truth. . . . You know him, for he lives *with you* and will be in you. (John 14:16–17).

A family tradition that includes regular time spent around a family altar strengthens its connections with God as well as with each other. As family members gather around the family altar, they have God's promise of help in strengthening *the family spirit.*

> You received the Spirit of sonship. And by him we cry, *"Abba,* Father." The Spirit himself

testifies with *our spirit* that *we* are God's children. (Rom. 8:15–16)

Imagine this! God actually lives in your house and controls the weather for you.

> In him you too are being built together to become a dwelling in which God lives by his Spirit. (Eph. 2:22)

Knowing that God's Spirit is in the room with you certainly affects your mood toward each other. Why not set an empty chair there to remind the family that Jesus is with you?

> When you are assembled in the name of our Lord Jesus, . . . the power of our Lord Jesus *is present*. (1 Cor. 5:4)

God promises to keep your family unit protected from the forces of evil as you gather together in His name. Then He can provide spiritual protection for the family spirit against bad weather—protection for the vital relationships that make up the connecting places within the family.

> Finally, be strong in the Lord and in his mighty power. Put on the full armor of God so that you can take your stand against the devil's schemes. For our struggle is not against flesh and blood, but . . . against the powers of this dark world and against the spiritual forces of evil in the heavenly realms. (Eph. 6:11–12)

The family altar can be an actual place in your home, set aside for renewing the family spirit. Your family can gather around this altar each day for devotions and for sharing each other's lives as the Spring family did. This can be something scheduled into your family's lifestyle and made a top priority. Such time together can grow to be something very special—a "sacred" time.

God Can Control the Weather from Anywhere

Different schedules and pressures often make family altar time hard to maintain. Rather than limit family time because of scheduling problems, why not expand the family altar? Christ's promise to be with us is not limited to a place. No matter where it is, whenever two or three are gathered in His name, He will be there with them (Matt. 18:20).

Whenever two, three, or more members of your family are together, use that as an opportunity to work on renewing the family spirit. Acknowledge God's presence often when you are together, and be creative with your desire to strengthen your family ties around the family altar. Make it a portable altar and take it with you wherever you go.

The Portable Family Altar: Watching TV

The program was over and a commercial demanded attention. The Spring family started watching with glazed eyes when Rose observed, "Wow! They can make it feel so romantic to drink together!" "That's true," Elaine added. "Sex is used to sell their product. Do you think that is good?" "I see it all the time," Sonny chimed in. "I didn't notice anything until my bright sister make her observation." There was a pause, and then Robert turned off the TV and asked, "Just what messages have you gotten from TV about sex?" Rose thought for a minute and then said with hesitation, "Well . . . it seems that sex is just there for a person's pleasure." Sonny added, "It's just natural. People go to bed if they like each other." "Is that a good way of behaving?" Elaine asked. "I never thought about it much," said Rose, "but that puts sex in the same category as playing a game together. It sure doesn't make it very special!" "That's right," Elaine broke in. "I believe God gave us the sexual emotions so that we could bond with each other. That's how this family was formed," she said as she winked at Robert. "You know," Sonny exclaimed, "I never thought of that! If sex is just another way to have fun, how can it have power to hold families together?" "That's right," Robert concluded. "Casual sex isn't a very good way to hold families together!"

Most people watch TV in silence, fuzzing out during commercials. Use this as family time together. Take the images and values that are presented and use the opportunity to share ideas and values. Shut off the TV as the Spring family did and talk over reactions to the messages given by the program. Perhaps you can show religiously oriented videos as part of family time.

The Portable Family Altar: Taking a Drive

Family members are often in the car together. It may be a vacation trip together or perhaps a shorter weekend outing. Certainly there are shorter trips to school functions, children's activities, or even grocery shopping. Instead of seeing the drive as boring, with everyone buried in private thought, see it as an opportunity to make contact with each other.

The Portable Family Altar: Eating Out

Eating out is often a rushed affair with little conversation. Make this also an opportunity to work on the family ties. Don't forget a prayer together. Have fun focusing on one of the family members for that evening.

The Portable Family Altar: A Hot-Air Balloon

"Mommy! Daddy!" Dawn shouted with excitement, "I can see way down. Cars look so tiny down there." Up in the balloon the rest of the family smiled at Dawn's energy. They were all having fun, soaring high above the earth. This was a trip the family would never forget. "Thank you, thank you for taking us!" Sonny and Rose chimed in. "You are the best parents in the whole world!" Robert and Elaine looked at each other and smiled happily. Something special passed between them at that moment—a warmth, closeness, and love. Elaine could not help but exclaim, "Let's thank God for the love He has given to our family!" They joined hands, and Robert offered a prayer of thanksgiving as the balloon rose even higher in the sky.

On the way home after everyone had talked about the experience, Robert used the balloon ride as family altar time. The gondola, he said, showed that they were all in the family together and would all be affected by the forces that controlled the mood of the family.

"The balloon is the structure of the family— the trust we have for each other. If the structure is good, the balloon will hold air, but if it gets ripped apart by distrust, then the family balloon cannot get off the ground. Lies and deceit rip apart this trust, so let's make a promise to each other that we will be truthful."

Robert then pointed out that he had not always been truthful, especially in the area of money, and that the deceit was hard on the family. "I have learned something very important that I want all of you to follow. It is never right to be dishonest."

"The burner is critical to the family balloon," he continued. "When the burner is ignited, it warms up the air and lifts the balloon off the ground. When the burner is shut down, the air in the envelope cools, and the balloon drops to the ground."

"When we show respect to each other," Robert continued as he smiled at Dawn, "it is like two spirits touching, sparking a flame of love that warms up the atmosphere of the envelope. Then our family balloon soars high in the sky. But when we show disrespect," Robert pointed out as he contorted his face into a fake frown at Dawn, "the burner goes out and the mood of the family shifts downward."

"My Sunday school teacher said that the Holy Spirit is like a fire," Rose broke in. "The Holy Spirit is the fire that gets the burner going when we are upset with each other. He helps get us back together." Elaine smiled with pride at Rose and said, "Say, that is good thinking! The Holy Spirit brings Jesus' love back into our lives. He lets us know that Jesus forgives us and helps us to forgive each other. That's what we need to get us together again."

"What do you think happens if the burner stays off too long?" Robert asked. Sonny immediately replied, "The balloon will crash down into the ground." "That's right," Robert said as he ruffled his son's hair. "If you stay upset at one of us too long, bad things will start happening to the family balloon. Gradually we start having bad feelings toward each other and stay mad longer." "So," Elaine added, "your father and I have agreed that from now on, we will never go to bed angry at each other. We want you to make that promise too."

The Portable Family Altar: Going to Church

One of the problems of the family unit in our culture is that it so often becomes an isolated, "nuclear" family.

Given the powerful nature of the forces that the family unit faces both within and without, the family needs a source of strength and nurture.

The congregation can provide this resource by becoming an extended family for all of its members. First, it can keep the nuclear family from being isolated by bringing the Word that connects each believer not only to God but to all of God's family. The message of forgiveness in Jesus Christ is not a message that leaves us alone and disconnected. We have been adopted into the family of God Himself. In this family even the most isolated believer is never a believer alone. Jesus Christ has made all His people into family members (John 1:12–13; Mark 3:34–35).

The church is not just a building where individuals go to worship God in isolation. The church is a community of believers—a fellowship that has a spirit of its own. And the church is also portable; it is not just a building. The church is wherever members are gathered together.

At Robert and Elaine's suggestion, their congregation began to emphasize Sunday as the "day for God's family." First there was a time for donuts, coffee, and juice. Then came times for study, for discussion, for singing, for worship, for eating, for activities, for fellowship, for fun, and for stories from the "old-timers." Often the congregation would block out Sunday morning and part of the afternoon for "family altar time" for the church family. There would always be some activity that would be started on Sunday but that each family would have to finish one evening during the week. This past Sunday each family started making a banner that would express their family history. The Spring family decided to put weather patterns on their banner. At home they had fun with the project, deciding to make two banners. The first showed lots of stormy turbulence. The second one showed a

stormy turbulence. The second one showed a strong system of fair weather. Of course, the cross of Christ was in the center of the second banner.

The Lasting Effect of a Good Spirit

Do you ever wonder what true happiness really is? Have you ever observed people who are wealthy and powerful yet seem to be miserable and unhappy? "Instead, be filled with the Spirit. . . . Sing and make music in your heart to the Lord. . . . Submit to one another out of reverence for Christ" (Eph. 5:18–21). This is true happiness.

A person will never forget the love of someone who has deeply touched his/her spirit. Such moments remain real and vivid many years later. Time seems to stand still for such spiritual connections.

It was a birthday celebration in the Spring home. Rose was 16 years old. She was excited about all the presents but wanted to hurry with the family celebration so she could go with her daddy to get her driver's license. Elaine was careful to keep her present until the end. Inside a carefully wrapped package was a little girl's outfit. As the rest of the family asked why such a present, Rose and her mother just paused for a moment and looked at each other. Both were propelled back 10 years earlier when Rose was six. Elaine had taken off from work and had driven with Rose to a neighboring city to buy that outfit. Both had no trouble remembering that special day. Rose went over and hugged her mother and whispered, "You'll always be my mommy!" Elaine held on tight as warm tears formed in her eyes.

If you see anyone who deeply touched you 10 years

earlier, you reexperience that depth. You carry each of these deep, spiritual connections with you for the rest of your life—and beyond. "Now these three remain: faith, hope and love. But the greatest of these is love" (1 Cor. 13:13).

When the family keeps the atmosphere free and open, the spirit grows. The direction of a good spirit is always upward and outward (▲). It can touch the lives of many other people.

The upward flow of a good spirit produces fruits of *lasting* value. This good spirit moves beyond its original relationship and extends to many other relationships and persons, for "love never ends" (1 Cor. 13:8 RSV). Long after a good spirit has been formed, it continues to be active. It contains positive energy that spills over to produce fair weather in other relationships. I know that firsthand.

> My mother has been dead for a number of years, and I still think about her and miss her. Thoughts of her and of the love of God she so freely shared still arouse a deep warmth and connectedness within me, leaving a sense of adequacy and worth. My wife Kathy now lives in this place of warmth in my spirit, special and precious to its daily life! My warmth and caring for others flow from this place deep within. It is in this spirit that I write.
>
> "May the God of hope fill you with all joy and peace as you trust in him, so that you may overflow with hope by the power of the Holy Spirit" (Rom. 15:13).

Chapter 8: Weather Control Activities

1. The family needs a place where it can regularly strengthen the *family ties*. I know of no better place than

around the family altar. First, develop this altar as a physical location in your home. Make it a comfortable, attractive space where the family can gather and spend some time together. Make it a special, sacred place that all members will look back on with warmth, security, and depth, remembering the good discussions that took place there. Decide on such a place before you go on to the next step, and prepare that place by actually making an altar there, perhaps with candles and a cross.

2. Next, you need a time (at least 10 minutes) when the family will gather around the altar each day for devotions and conversation. Also plan an extended time (at least a half-hour) one day a week. Decide on such a time before you go on.

3. Begin with a devotion each time. Develop the spirit so that spontaneous comments can be made, even during the devotional time, so that boredom or disinterest does not set in. Relate the devotion to the life of the family and its members. Have a time for prayer for anyone or anything of concern by family members.

4. Put one member of the family in charge of bringing up a topic of conversation each evening. Have that person start by expressing some feeling or concern going on in his/her life so that the family can stay connected with each other.

5. Always close the family altar time with the question, "Does anyone have anything they need to express?" This will prevent hurt feelings from being carried over to the next day. Then leave after everyone has touched each other in some way.

6. After developing the family altar at home, think creatively about the portable family altar. List all the times when family members are naturally together. Think of ways in which you can make these times part of the family altar.

7. Take seriously the concept that you can positively affect the weather around your home by developing a family lifestyle that keeps the communication open with God

and with each other. It will not happen naturally. There are too many schedules, too much TV, too many outside forces. As you see the importance of family time, make that time. Make it prime time.

Notes

1. The development of the ritual surrounding the family altar is important for working on the family ties, but it is also important for keeping the channels of communication open so that when sensitive and hurtful issues arise, there will be a way of talking them over. Such rituals can naturally lead to heart-to-heart talks, since the mood (spirit) is set for such conversations. The family spirit just does not get into the same trouble if such talks regularly occur.

2. The church can help by supporting the family altar. The local congregation can make the development of the family altar one of its priorities and help families actually start this tradition. Congregations can help, for example, by providing stimulating materials to be used around the family altar.

3. Even though this book was written for the family unit, virtually everything that appears in it can also be applied to the church family. The same spiritual dynamics occur there, and certainly the spirit of each congregation (its *family spirit*) must also be worked on regularly. Most of the ideas will also apply to the work place and to friendships, for these too have a shared space and an atmosphere.

Renewing the Family Spirit

Video Course

To help you renew your family's spirit within a group or congregational setting, Concordia Video has developed an in-depth video study course. The course, also titled *Renewing the Family Spirit,* presents an innovative yet practical guide to understanding and resolving differences in the everyday life of your family and others in the group. You and other families will better understand Gospel-based family relationships as members reveal and heal their differences to renew and strengthen the family spirit.

The course contains a detailed leaders guide and three videocassettes with all the support materials for eight 60-minute sessions. This adaptable course can be expanded to 16 weeks or more. It can also be used for family weekend retreats. And you do not have to be an expert to lead the course. All the materials you will need to lead this course successfully have been carefully prepared and included for you. If you are a pastor or member of a church or group interested and concerned about encouraging a God-supported spirit in today's families, give serious consideration to this important and helpful video course.

For a free brochure on the *Renewing the Family Spirit* video course (and other family life materials on video), write to

> Good News for Families
> Renewing the Family Spirit Video
> Concordia Publishing House
> 3558 South Jefferson Ave.
> St. Louis, MO 63118

BV 4526.2 .L83 1989
Ludwig, David J.
Renewing the family spirit

BV 4526.2 .L83 1989
Ludwig, David J.
Renewing the family spirit

90l2

SEP

DATE DUE	BORROWER'S NAME	ROOM NUMBER
901230	IL: 911 6314	
AUG 2 6 1991	TIM IHSSEN	
SEP 13 '91		